Contents

✎ **KU-164-665**

Tony Buzan

Make the Most of Your Mind

illustrated by Richard Fowler

Pan Books London and Sydney

First published 1977 by Colt Books Ltd
This edition published 1981 by Pan Books Ltd,
Cavaye Place, London SW10 9PG
2nd printing 1981
© Tony Buzan 1977
Illustrations © Colt Books Ltd 1977
ISBN 0 330 26230 0
Reproduced, printed and bound in Great Britain by
Cox & Wyman Ltd, Reading

Acknowledgements

I would like to thank those people who have specially helped to make this book possible: Joseph Adams, Ken Adams, Mortimer Adler, Professor Zita Albes, Mrs. Bakhtiar, David Bolton, Mark Brown, Helga Buechner, John Bush, Joy Buttery, Barry Buzan, Gordon Buzan, Jean Buzan, Jeremy Cartland, Derek Chapman, Bill Chester, Gina Chester, Bernard Chibnall, Pan Collins, Paul Collins, Bernard Cowley, Keith Davis, Terry Dixon, Costas Florides, Lorraine Gill, Robert Heller, Harold Hemming, Moofy Hemming, Brian Helweg Larsen, Hermione Lovel, Alexander Luria, Joe McMahon, Anette McGee, John McNulty, Heinz Norden, Robert Ornstein, Anne Parks, Michael Ronan, Peter Russell, Robin Sales, John Staheli, Louisa Service, Caroline Shott, Chris Stevens, Aida Svendsen, Susan Thame, Nancy Thomas, Robert Thouless, Nicholas Wade, Bill Watts, Brian Wills, Robert Yeatman.

Introduction

Your Brain's Potential

Your brain is like a sleeping giant. During recent years, researches in psychology, education, biochemistry, physics and mathematics have shown that the potential of your brain is far greater than was generally imagined. Even the commonly heard statement that "on average we use only 1% of our brains" may well be wrong because it now seems that we use even less than 1% — which means that an enormous amount of your capability is still available for development.

Make the Most of Your Mind is designed to help you develop that astounding untapped potential. The first chapter outlines some of the most recent findings about your brain, including news from the most exciting "brain frontier": the different mental functions of the left and right sides of your brain. These discoveries and other facts about the structure of your brain and the number of connective patterns it can make are described in a way that will help you use the information to improve your own mental performance.

The next three chapters deal with: memory and how you can improve your basic capacity as well as your special abilities for remembering facts, names and faces; listening and how to select "keys" that help you to concentrate; and seeing, a chapter that concentrates on new findings about your eyes' ability to see more clearly, more analytically, more extensively — and faster. Your visual capacity is directly related to reading and speed reading. Diagrams show how your eyes normally function and how this function can be enormously improved, giving automatic increases in reading speed and efficiency.

The information from these early chapters is next applied to note-making and the creative organization of thought. Methods for reducing the volume of notes you make are outlined and these are combined with other techniques to help you make note-making more effective. With this new note-making ability, creativity can also be enhanced. Techniques like "brain patterning" are included with examples and exercises that will help you to improve your own creative thinking.

The last two chapters give a simple introduction to those two areas that so often cause people mental stress: numbers and logic.

The numeracy chapter shows that everyone has a latent mathematical ability, regardless of what he or she may have been told, and outlines simple techniques for handling addition, subtraction, multiplication and division more confidently. The chapter also includes some fast-calculating techniques that will enable you to perform mental gymnastics in your head within seconds, while others spend minutes with pen and paper.

The final chapter is on logic and analysis. It outlines with examples, ten basic areas of logical thinking in which you can improve your ability to analyse, to make judgements, and to present your own thoughts clearly.

Developing Your Approach

Some readers may wish to make a major project of improving themselves, and may decide to devote considerable time and effort to the project. Others may wish to turn to this book for occasional help in areas where they need special attention.

Both approaches are completely valid, and can be compared with approaches to sports. If you wish to become a champion, complete dedication is necessary, with daily work and practice. If you wish to become an adequate "social" tennis player, basic information is required, plus occasional attention to footwork, angle of the racket, smoothness of strokes; such small adjustments can make major differences to performance. It is the same with your brain. Even a slight adjustment to the way in which you use your brain can produce dramatic results.

Whether you use *Make the Most of Your Mind* in order to excel or to improve your general mental performance, the book will give you a new self-awareness and confidence whenever you have to use your ability to think.

Chapter Design

Each chapter is constructed to make it easy for you to scan, read and remember. At the beginning of each chapter is a brief summary of the contents. After each summary is an even shorter "key word" summary which extracts the main idea-words from the chapter. Included in some of the chapters are games and tests that will enable you to judge and analyse your own performance. In many of these games and tests there is no scoring at all. In those items which are scored, the score is judged neither "bad" nor "good"; it simply serves as a baseline from which you are able to improve, no matter where you start.

At the end of each chapter are "brain pattern" summaries of the contents of the chapter. You can think of these brain pattern summaries as "mental maps" of the information you have just read. Each brain pattern contains a central word or image that summarizes the main idea of the chapter. Radiating from this centre are main key-words and images that summarize the most important sub-sections of the chapter, and radiating from these main "spokes" are minor key words and key images from the other areas of importance within the chapter.

The advantage of these brain patterns is that they can summarize, on one page, a connected mental image of all the most important parts of the chapter. You will find, after studying them, that your memory of what you have read will be greatly improved. These brain patterns are in no way final, and if you wish to add your own words and images to them it will be to your advantage.

At the end of each chapter is a blank page or two for your notes. As you read *Make the Most of Your Mind* you may find ideas and memories pop into your own mind. Jot these down in the appropriate place, and build up an even more complete summary of knowledge about each chapter. On these personal note pages you can include new information you gather from newspapers, books, radio or television.

Further Reading

At the very end of the book is a list of recommended books for further reading. This is divided into three sections:

1. general reading

2. novels

3. psychology/practical

These books, whether they are more academic or more entertaining, will provide you with additional information about your brain, as well as with much food for further thought.

General Advice

When reading this or most other books, it is advisable to scan the book before settling down to an "in-depth" reading. As one reader put it: "Case the joint before going in and getting what you want"! You will find that scanning enables you to get a more complete grasp of the entire subject, making in-depth reading that much easier.

It is advisable to skip any difficult areas, going back to them at a later stage, when the additional information that you have gathered from the rest of the book will make the difficult areas easier to understand.

Developing Your Potential

Why is so little of the brain's potential ability used?

One of the main reasons is that until only recently we have known very little about the brain and the way it works. Many of the problems we encounter in the use of our mental abilities do not result from any lack in the brain's basic capacity but from inadequate knowledge of its potential and how to use it. Our increasing understanding of the structure of the brain and the way it functions can help us to overcome both this difficulty and the lack of confidence so many of us experience in making the most of the ability we already possess.

WHAT WERE YOU TAUGHT?

In your formal schooling you were no doubt taught a wide range of academic subjects. Most people find that despite this they were taught very little about how they and their minds work. The following "Yes/No" questions will give you an idea of what you may have missed. Record your answers as you go along.

In your formal education were you taught about:

1. the major left/right divisions of your brain?

    Yes/No

2. the general structure of your brain and its brain cells?   Yes/No

3. the mathematical, memory, and learning potential of your brain?   Yes/No

4. the way your memory changes during learning?

    Yes/No

5. the way your memory changes after learning?

    Yes/No

6. special memory systems for improving all kinds of recall?   Yes/No

7. how to improve your listening ability?

    Yes/No

8. the way in which your eyes move when they take in information?   Yes/No

9. the way in which eyes can be taught to take in more information than they normally do?

    Yes/No

10. how visual guides can increase your reading speed?   Yes/No

11. the nature of comprehension and how this can be improved?   Yes/No

12. shorthand techniques?   Yes/No

13. the way in which words and images "work" in your mind?   Yes/No

14. note-making techniques allowing you to form "mental pictures" of your thoughts?

    Yes/No

15. how to prepare completely for, and write, examinations?   Yes/No

16. how to plan and present reports, speeches and
    presentations?   Yes/No

17. the meaning of creativity?   Yes/No

18. the potential of the average brain's creativity?
                                             Yes/No

19. special techniques for vastly speeding up add-
    ition, subtraction, multiplication, and division?
                                             Yes/No

20. techniques for analysing arguments in order to
    enable you to pick out the logical flaws?
                                             Yes/No

Most people answer "Yes" to only a very few of these questions.
Many answer "Yes" to none of them. One of the purposes of
this book is to correct this imbalance.

YOUR PROBLEMS

In the following space note down, *in detail,* all the problems
you have in using your brain. Make sure you are honest with
yourself and that you leave nothing out. The more you bring
the problems to light, the easier it will be for you to solve them
as you progress through the book.

The Problems

No matter how many you wrote down, don't worry. Although your own list and the following list of other people's problems might seem a little forbidding, there is still hope, for the brain is capable of performing more than adequately, even when we place it under the pressures that give rise to many of these problems.

What the lists signify is that we have not really been given enough information about how our brains work. Most of us can be compared with the unfortunate owner of a Rolls-Royce who, not knowing how the machine operates, mistakenly lubricates it with water, and then blames it for not working.

Recently, so much new light has been shed on the structure of your brain that we now *know* it can be helped to function far more effectively. The Rolls-Royce does work, and there are better ways of lubricating its ability.

age	content	hierarchies
aims	continuity	humour
alertness	conversation	imagery
amount	credibility	imagination
analogies	decisiveness	impatience
analysis	definition	inhibition
anxiety	dictation	initiation
appreciation	discipline	intelligence
aptitude	distraction	interest
assessment	dyslexia	interpretation
assimilation	education	interrogation
association	ego	interviewing
atmosphere	emotions	intuition
attention	environment	irrelevance
attitude	expression	languages
back-skipping	fatigue	layout
bias	fear	laziness
bio-rhythms	feedback	learning
boredom	fitness	lighting
clarity	flexibility	listening
classifying	fluency	logic
comfort	frustration	meetings
communication	getting down to it	memory
complication	goals	mental blocks
conflict	goal-setting	mental set
confidence	health	methodology

mis-linking
motivation
nerves
noise
note taking
numbers
objectives
objectivity
ordering
organization
panic
perception
persuasion
planning
prejudice
preparation
presentation
pressure
priorities
problem-solving

rapport
rationalization
reading
reassembling
recalling
regression
rejection
relaxation
retention
reviewing
rhythm
scanning
selection
sequencing
skipping
sleep
speaking
speed
spelling
stickability

stopping
stress
study-reading
style
sub-vocalization
temperature
tension
thinking ahead/back
time
typography
uncertainty
understanding
verbosity
vision
visualizing
vocabulary
vocalization
will-power
writing

The problems listed above are a summary of the problems given by people attending **Learning** Methods Group courses. They include businessmen, university students, housewives, children, politicians, teachers and professors. No matter what walk of life the people came from, the pattern of their problems was very similar. Most of these problems were significantly reduced when they were able to apply to the problems the basic information about their brains which is outlined in the following chapters.

1. Your Brain

What is the real potential of your brain, and what is its physical nature? In this chapter the early history of thought on the brain is briefly introduced, and then three of the latest and most significant findings about your brain are described: the left and right sides of your brain; the physical structure and connection patterns of your individual brain cells; and the number of electrochemical interactions continually taking place in your brain. The last section of the chapter discusses the question of mental ability in relation to age and suggests that you *can* teach an old dog new tricks.

KEY WORD SUMMARY

> History — brain
>
> Left and right sides
>
> Brain cells
>
> Brain connections
>
> Electrochemical interactions
>
> Your potential
>
> Improving with age

From Past to Present

Did you know that your brain is divided into two halves? And furthermore did you know that those two halves are two separate brains?

As little as two thousand years ago mankind knew virtually nothing about the brain. Before the Greeks, the mind was not even considered to be part of the human body but was thought to exist as some form of vapour, gas or disembodied spirit.

Surprisingly, the Greeks did not get us that much farther, and even Aristotle, their most famous philosophical thinker and the founder of modern science, concluded after extensive investigations that the centre of sensation and memory was located in the heart. From the time of the Greeks to the beginning of the Renaissance there was virtually no progress at all. During the Renaissance, a period of great intellectual awakening, it was finally realized that the centre of thought and consciousness was located in the head, but the brain remained a mystery.

It was not until the 20th century that the really great strides forward were made in our understanding of our own brains, and many people still assume that it was in the first half of the century that the greatest advances were made. On the contrary, through the 1930s and 1940s we still believed the brain to be a simple machine, operating much like the very first computers, in which a few basic messages went in, were placed in the appropriate boxes, and that that was all there was to it. This model of the brain was common in first-year psychology and educational textbooks until the late 1950s.

It was not until very recently that the really major breakthroughs were made. These developments are so significant that they are already changing the foundations of psychology and education, and are emphasizing a fact sensed by many but until now impossible to "prove": that the average brain is far more capable than we ever believed.

Two findings stand out as particularly significant.

Your Left and Right Brain

For some time it has been known that the brain is divided into two sides, left and right. It has also been known that if damage is done to the left side of the brain, the right side of the body tends to become paralysed, and correspondingly that if damage is done to the right side of the brain, the left side of the body tends to become paralysed. In other words, each side of your brain controls the opposite side of your body.

The recent research of Professor Robert Ornstein of the University of California has thrown more light on the different activities handled by each side of the brain.

Starting with the realization that the two halves of the brain are biologically similar and can more realistically be thought of as two identical brains working in harmony, rather than as one brain divided into two, Professor Ornstein decided to find out if each of our separate brains handles different intellectual activities in addition to the different physical activities.

Placing special caps for measuring brain waves on some of his students, he asked them to do different kinds of mental tasks. They were asked to add lists of numbers, write formal letters and essays, arrange coloured blocks, analyse logically, and think "daydreamy" thoughts. All the time these activities were being performed, Professor Ornstein was measuring the brain waves coming from the two halves of each person's brain.

His findings were both surprising and significant: that in general the left brain handles the following mental activities:

1. mathematics
2. language
3. logic
4. analysis
5. writing
6. and other similar activities

and that the right side of the brain handles very different activities:

1. imagination
2. colour
3. music
4. rhythm
5. daydreaming
6. and other similar activities

Ornstein also found that people who had been trained to use one side of their brain more or less exclusively were relatively unable to use the other side, both in general and in those special situations where the activities specifically related to the other side were particularly needed.

Even more significantly, Ornstein found that when the "weaker" of the two brains was stimulated and encouraged to work in co-operation with the stronger side, the end result was a great increase in overall ability and effectiveness.

These increases were larger than Ornstein anticipated: he had expected that by encouraging the weaker side to work in conjunction with the stronger side, he would get an increase of the type: 1 side + 1 side = twice as effective a performance. The actual result showed that the brain can sometimes work in a way different from the standard mathematics, for when one side was "added" to the other side, the result was often five to ten times more effective.

Ornstein's findings have special significance for those of us educated in the West, for most of us have been trained in the three Rs: reading, writing and arithmetic — left-brain, left-brain, left-brain. We have traditionally considered the student who is artistically talented, musical, good with his hands and a bit "dreamy", to be unintelligent, stupid, non-university material and "thick". All the evidence now suggests that this has been a mistake, and that the more creative or artistic person is just as "intelligent" as the more academic person.

The Artist and the Scientist

This work has been further supported by an investigation into those people normally considered to be the great artists and scientists. Einstein, for instance, often considered to be the greatest scientist of his time, was not simply a fuzzy-headed mathematical physicist whose brain was full of numbers and formulae. Records show that he failed mathematics at school and that he was nearly thrown out of college for daydreaming.

According to Einstein himself, he discovered his theory of relativity not seated in front of his desk, but while lying on a hill one summer day.

As he looked up with half-closed eyes, the sun dappled through his eyelashes, breaking into thousands of tiny sunbeams. Einstein wondered what it would be like to go for a ride on one of those sunbeams, and in his imagination took himself on a journey through the universe. His imagination took him to a place where his formal training in physics told him he should not be. Concerned about this, he went back to his blackboard, and believing his imagination to be more correct that his formal training, worked out a new mathematics to explain the truth of what his brain had told

R   L

Images   Words

Rhythm   Numbers

Colour   Logic

Daydreaming   Analysis

$1+1 \neq 2$

$$1+1=5$$
and more

Your brain is divided into two separate brains. The left brain takes as its domain the following mental activities: Words, numbers, logic and analysis. The right brain takes as its domain: Images, colour and daydreaming, etc. You have both "scientific" *and* "artistic" abilities.

25

him. Looking back we can see that he was actually using both sides of his brain to an exceptional degree, the right side of his brain producing the beautiful imagined journey, and the left side of his brain being used to develop the new physics and mathematics, and to provide a formal framework for the image he had created. This combination provided mankind with one of the most significant theories of all time.

Similarly, studies of the great artists have shown that they were not slap-happy splashers of colour on canvas. Investigation of the notebooks of such famous painters as Klee, Cézanne and Picasso, have shown them to be exceptionally mathematical and geometrical in their descriptions of what they are trying to do, outlining in intricate detail the specific inter-relationships they are trying to make with colour, form and line. Again and again investigation shows that the great minds have been mistakenly labelled either "artistic" or "scientific" when in fact they were both.

Perhaps the best example of this is the man considered by many to have one of the greatest brains of all time: Leonardo da Vinci. Leonardo's renown as history's most complete man is based on the very fact that he excelled in his mathematical, linguistic, logical and analytical faculties, while excelling in his ability to use imagination, colour, rhythm and form.

The intelligent conclusion to be drawn from Ornstein's work is that each one of us is potentially both exceptionally scientific and exceptionally artistic. If we are at the moment lop-sided it is not because of an inherent disability, but simply because one side of our brain has not been given as much opportunity to develop as the other.

The Structure of Your Brain

The second new and significant piece of information about our brains was discovered by Professor Pyotr Anokhin, the protégé and direct descendant of Pavlov in psychology.

For centuries, the brain had been considered as merely a "three-and-a-half-pound lump of grey matter". With the development of the microscope it was discovered that the brain's crumpled outer layer was far more complex than had been previously believed, and that it was composed of many thousands of intricate nerve and blood pathways.

Albert Einstein, the renowned physicist and mathematician, did *not* get his ideas only from the left or mathematical side of his brain. He imagined many of the laws of the universe and then applied his mathematical ability to that initial inspirational image.

As microscopy continued to improve, so did our knowledge of the structure of the brain. It was soon realized that each brain was composed of millions of tiny cells called neurons. In a scientific saga similar to that of astronomy — in which more has been discovered, the more powerful our measuring instruments have become — scientists next discovered that each brain cell was like a tiny octopus, having a centre, or nucleus, and a large number of little tentacles radiating in all directions from it.

Continuing on their magnification journey, the scientists found that each of these tentacles had thousands of tiny protuberances, much like the suction pads on the tentacles of the octopus, but protruding from all sides of the tentacle.

By this stage in the investigation they had calculated that the average brain contained a staggering number of individual neurons: 10,000 million!

It was thought for a while that the number of brain cells determined the comparative intelligence of the person, but this belief was soon laid to rest when it was found that many people with "large" brains had been apparently unintelligent, whereas a number of people with "small" brains had shown considerable intelligence.

Connections and Pathways in Your Brain

Professor Anokhin was among the first to realize that it was not the number of brain cells that determined intelligence but something to do with the little protuberances on the brain cells' tentacles. He found that each protuberance was connected to at least one other, and by means of electro-chemical impulses these two could form little patterns with other individuals and other groups. As he progressed, Anokhin realized that each brain was a fantastic interlinking of patterns formed by the thousands of protuberances on the many arms of the many millions of brain cells.

In the last year of his life, Professor Anokhin calculated the number of connections and pathways that could be made by a normal brain. He emphasized, as a scientist, that his estimate was conservative, and concluded his last public statement by saying he was convinced that no man was alive or had ever lived who even approached the full use of his brain. The

Scientists have discovered that each brain contains 10,000 million brain cells. Each one of these brain cells is like a tiny octopus, with many connection points on each of the many arms. This artist's impression gives you an idea of what each of these minute cells is like.

number he calculated is still staggering scientists and teachers alike:

1 followed by

10 MILLION KILOMETRES

of standard typewritten noughts!

Unlimited Potential?

Ornstein's findings about our artistic and academic abilities, and Anokhin's findings about the almost limitless potential of our minds to form patterns and connections, have confirmed the current trend in thought that everyone's brain is much better than it has been given credit for, and that most of the problems we experience with the use of our brains are not because of any fundamental inability but because we have so far not received enough information about ourselves and the way we work.

Improving with age

One final bit of good news about our brains has come from the research of Professor Mark Rosenzweig and others.

For far too long it has been assumed that the brain declines with age, reaching a peak between the ages of 18 and 24, and deteriorating steadily from then on. This decline was held to include most mental abilities — among them recall, retention, numerical ability, creativity, alertness and vocabulary. These beliefs were supported by common sayings such as "You can't teach an old dog new tricks".

All of these mistaken beliefs can now be comfortably laid to rest. Professor Rosenzweig has shown that if the brain is stimulated, *no matter at what age,* it will physically grow more protuberances on each brain cell's tentacles, and that these protuberances will increase the total number of connections within the human brain.

Apart from these scientific findings, history is dotted with great minds who showed that ability was not dependent on age: among them Gauguin, who did not really start to paint until his 35th year; Michelangelo, who was producing great works of sculpture, art and writing into his 80th year; Haydn, who wrote some of his most beautiful music in the latter years of his life; and more recently again, Picasso, who was producing copiously into his nineties.

Evidence is also found in other societies, in which the elder members of the community were always considered to be the "Wise Men", a description which covered not only their knowledge and experience, but also their ability to use the knowledge they had.

In the light of all this, the old contention that we lose brain cells continually throughout our lives and that this causes serious mental decline fades into insignificance. Apart from the fact that we can generate new connections far more rapidly than the average loss of brain cells, it can also be shown that even if we lose 10,000 brain cells a day from the time we are born, we have started with so many that the total number lost by the age of 80 would be less than 3%.

Your Brain—Some Comparisons

The brain is often compared with machines and electrical systems, but what we now know about the brain makes this pretty hard on the machines. It has been calculated, for instance, that the entire network of the world's telephone systems, if properly compared to your brain, would occupy a part of it the size of an ordinary garden pea.

It has also been discovered by Professor D. Samuel of The Weizmann Institute in Israel that at any given moment there are between 100,000 and a million chemical reactions taking place in your brain.

We have really just begun to realize that the human brain is a biological supercomputer, and that we are even now still only on the threshold of discovering its extraordinary abilities. Among our first priorities must be an exploration of the way it functions, and the development of exercises or techniques that will enable it to operate more naturally and effectively. This can be most usefully started by first looking at the workings of our memory and our basic senses, and then adapting our knowledge of the brain to help every sense to function more smoothly and easily.

The complexity of the world's entire telephone systems is equivalent to a part of your brain the size of an ordinary garden pea.

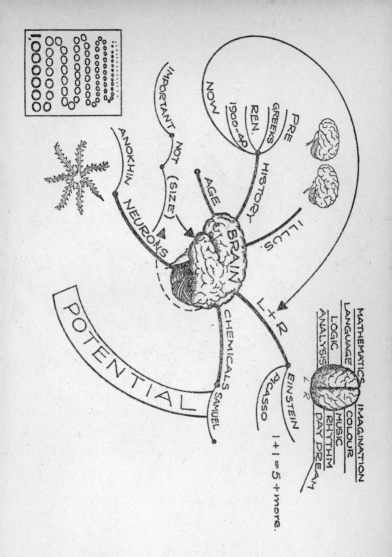

PERSONAL NOTES

2. Your Memory Can Be Better Than you Think

How often do you say, "It's on the tip of my tongue", or, "My head's like a sieve"? In this chapter evidence is given to show that your memory is better than you think. Special sections deal with self-checking, organizing your time to make sure that memory is maximized, and reviewing techniques to make sure that forgetting is held to a minimum. Outlines are given for solving the major memory problems: remembering names and faces, and remembering to link things together.

The final section explains how you can "set" yourself to remember.

KEY WORD SUMMARY

       Checking your current position

       Storing

       Retrieving

       Organizing time

       Linking

       Emphasizing

       Reviewing

       Link memory system

       Names and faces

       Setting yourself

Checking Your Current Position

Before reading this chapter, try a simple check. It's like Kim's Game which we played as children, trying to memorize the objects on a tray.

Opposite is a list of words (don't look at them yet!). When you have finished reading these instructions, read through the list at your normal speed, consciously trying to remember every word, one word at a time, *making sure you do not go back over any words you have read.* There are too many words in the entire list for you to remember them all, so the task is simply to remember as much as you can.

pay
head
turn
now
fee
field
the
of
left
and
to
of
which
the
will
once
and
more
clearly
Mao Tse-tung
together
inch
and
the
then
of
they
actual
of
and
case
the
repeat
same
other.

Now turn the page, without looking back, and answer the questions.

1. How many of the first six words in the list can you remember?

_____ _____ _____ _____ _____ _____

2. How many of the last six words can you remember?

_____ _____ _____ _____ _____ _____

3. Can you remember any word which appeared more than once?

4. Can you remember any word or group of words that was outstandingly different from all the others?

5. Can you remember any other words?

This little check on memory is designed to see not *how much* you remembered, but *how* you remembered. In the following pages a special section is devoted to improving any areas of weakness.

Memory Improves with age

"Difficulties with memory" are commonly mentioned by people when asked what problems they have in using their brains.

In fact, this has become almost institutionalized, and society now generally accepts that most of us have poor memories, and that memory declines as we get older. Some people even go so far as to congratulate themselves on their declining memory, and it is not uncommon to hear half apologetic, half self-satisfied conversations like "My memory is not nearly so good as it used to be", "Yes, I know exactly what you mean, mine's not so good any more either".

Actually, the reverse is true. To confirm this, let us look at the different aspects of memory: how memory changes as time progresses *while* we learn and *after* we have learnt, and how we can look after our memory in such a way as to make sure that it remembers what we want it to remember, and that it progressively *improves* with age.

Retention and Recall

Memory can be divided into two aspects: retention and recall. Retention is the ability of the mind to take in and store information. Recall is the ability to select from that vast store the special piece of information we need at any given time.

When people complain of having "bad memories", they do not really mean that their entire memory is bad, but normally that their ability to *recall* something is temporarily weak.

This is perhaps best exemplified by the "tip of the tongue" feeling. In this situation the person *knows* that he knows something and will say, "It's on the tip of my tongue, but I can't *remember* it." What he really means is that his brain has retained the information, but that he cannot at that moment *recall* it.

If a case is to be made for the improvement of memory (and for most people this means the improvement of their recall) it is necessary first to establish that the store of information is there to be drawn from. Fortunately, there is considerable evidence to support the suggestion that our brains do retain far more information than is generally thought — perhaps, even *all* of it.

Retention—the Evidence

1. DEATH-TYPE EXPERIENCES. When people have been confronted with a truck bearing down on them or have fallen off a cliff or nearly drowned, and have somehow miraculously survived, they have reported that their entire life flashed before them just before they lost consciousness. On further questioning, they have insisted that it was not just a few important events, but their *entire* life. These experiences are reported by people of all ages and races, and are often given with considerable embarrassment, because the individual, not knowing that the experience is common, thinks something is wrong with him.

2. CONVERSATION. Because normal conversation is so commonplace and automatic, we tend not to notice the complex process taking place. When you listen to another person talking, automatically understanding as the con-

versation progresses, your brain is doing the most fantastic piece of retain/recall manipulation, checking in its storage banks for every word uttered, comparing it with all the previous times that that word has been uttered, and then making a long series of sense-links to guarantee that you experience a smooth and continuous flow of understanding. The speed and subtlety of this process is so extraordinary that you don't even notice it. By comparison, the most sophisticated computer in the world will be left far behind your brain within two seconds.

3. DREAMS. Many people experience dreams in which characters and situations appear after they had been "forgotten" for as many as fifty years — old school friends, first loves and so on. The vision of these people and places in the dream is usually described as completely clear, and surprising in its accuracy of detail.

4. HYPNOSIS. Under competent supervision, people have been able to "unlock" memory banks, releasing entire sections of their lives which for some reason they had been unable to recollect. When these hypnotic releases take place, the recall is once again exceptionally clear, indicating that the storage process throughout has been extremely accurate.

5. SURPRISE STIMULUS. In these situations you suddenly see, hear, touch, taste or smell something which "triggers off" an entire series of connected memories.

Many people experience this when returning to areas in which they once lived but have long since left. One of the most common is a return to an early school, where one whiff of aromas from the kitchen can bring back extremely pleasant or unpleasant memories.

6. EXPERIMENTS. In Canada, Dr Wilder Penfield probed the brains of his patients with tiny electrodes, looking for areas in the brain that were causing these patients to have epileptic fits. The patients remained conscious throughout the procedure, and to his surprise Dr Penfield noted that sometimes when he excited the tiny electrode his patient would

suddenly start "re-living" experiences from previous years, ranging from childhood to the day before the testing.

This happened time and time again with different patients, and upon checking with relations and people who had been present at the "re-lived" experiences, Penfield found that the brain was somehow being stimulated to total sensory recall of the event. He found that these events seemed to be stored over the surface of the brain, and suggested that if we could find the right clues it might be possible to unlock every event of a lifetime.

7. PHYSIOLOGICAL EVIDENCE. The work done by Professor Anokhin and Rosenzweig suggests that the brain does have the physical capacity to store most of the information that is fed into it. Rosenzweig calculated that even if the brain were fed ten new bits of information every second for its entire life, it would be nowhere near full.

8. SPECIAL MEMORY SYSTEMS. Special memory systems have been used by stage magicians and professional memorizers for centuries. Experiments showed that by using these systems anyone could remember unconnected items in random, ordinary and reverse order, with complete accuracy, even though they were given each new piece of information at the rate of one every two seconds. Performance only dropped off when people became bored.

9. FAMOUS MEMORIZERS. The man most famous for having a "perfect memory" was a Russian called "S". S's memory was so good that if you asked what happened on a given day fifteen years before, he would pause for a moment and then respond with the question: "At what time?"!

"S" was studied for many years by the Russian psychologist Aleksandr Luria, who confirmed that somehow, at an early age, "S's" brain had "clicked" into natural methods for retaining and recalling everything in his life. In all other respects, including the structure and general functioning of his brain, "S" was apparently like any other human being.

Your Recall, and How it Works

Knowing that the storage capacity of the brain *is* so great, we can now turn our attention to the second aspect of memory: recall.

There are five main factors which assist your memory to recall:

1. primacy

2. recency

3. linking

4. outstandingness

5. review

1. PRIMACY. All other things being equal you will recall the beginning of events more than the middle of events, and will recall a first event more than continued repetitions of that event. Thus, in the little memory check at the beginning of this chapter, you will probably have recalled quite a few of the first six words: pay, head, turn, now, fee, field.

2. RECENCY. Again, all other factors being equal, you will tend to recall events which are very recent. In the list you may have recalled one or two of the last four or five words: case, the, repeat, same, other. In real life terms it shows that you will recall yesterday better than the day before that, the day before yesterday better than the day before it, and so on.

This tendency extends even into very old age, where people will be inclined to remember the events of early childhood and the events of recent days, but not so much of their middle years—even to the extent of confusing the generations of their own family.

3. LINKING. You will recall anything which is connected better than something which is disconnected. In the list you will therefore have remembered the repeated (linked to themselves) words: and, of, the.

Recall during learning. As this graph shows, when you are learning
something there are four main areas of highest recall: the beginning; the
end; things which are linked; and things which are outstanding.

43

If you pause for a moment to think about the way you normally recall something, you will realize that the answer does "pop up" when the right *connection* is made.

4. OUTSTANDINGNESS. You will more or less automatically be able to recall anything which is strange, unusual, out of context, or outstanding. In the list you will probably have recalled Mao Tse-tung, simply because it was so different from all the other words. In real life your experience will confirm that really outstanding events, whether good or bad, usually remain indelibly marked in your mind.

5. REVIEW. Many physiologists now believe that part of the ability to recall depends on the "strength of the brain pattern" laid down biologically and electrically. They emphasize that this strength is increased by repeating the memory pattern. In practical terms, this means that anything which is reviewed will tend to be more firmly lodged in the brain than something which is simply skimmed over once and left to recede.

Applying this Knowledge

The knowledge that the brain recalls first and last things best is useful in any learning situation, for it helps us to organize time in such a way as to increase recall. For example, if you study for four hours without a break, you will be giving yourself only one primacy and one recency situation, allowing your recall to sag in the middle. Breaking the four hours into more reasonable units will provide a greater number of "first and last" situations, and a consequent rise in recall. These time units have to be long enough to enable the mind to build up a rhythm, and short enough to prevent it from having too large a sag in the middle. Experience now indicates an ideal study time of between 10 and 45 minutes, depending on such things as the difficulty of the subject and your level of interest. Organizing learning periods in this way not only helps recall, but also leaves you far more rested at the end of the learning period, because in the breaks (which should normally be between two and five minutes) your mind has had a chance both to rest and to sort out the information it has been taking in during the learning period.

recall   10 to 45 minutes

Ideal study time. The ideal study time is between 10 and 45 minutes. This ensures that the beginning and end periods of recall are high, while also making sure that the middle period is not so long that it sags down.

The fact that linking assists recall can be applied in a number of ways. It is obviously vital for comprehension and understanding, and can be used with great effectiveness in note-making and the organization of study. You can assist yourself in learning by consciously looking for the links between the units of information which are being given to you. (The chapters on Note-Making and Creativity will help you to develop this concept further.)

Knowing that your brain recalls things which are outstanding, you can assist your recall by mentally trying to emphasize those areas you particularly want to remember. This means making things larger than life, giving them extra-bright or contrasting colours, and placing them in situations that make them "stand out". (Specific examples and techniques are expanded in the section dealing with special memory systems on page 48.) Outstandingness can also be applied to note-making situations.

The Importance of Review

Proper reviewing or revision does not mean a blind repetition of information, but means an organized series of special times for looking at information already understood. Normally, after only four or five reviews, the information being reviewed will enter the "long-term memory" — that part of your memory where information like your name, address and normal vocabulary is stored for immediate and automatic recall.

Review should be sensibly spaced out. This normally means that after a period of learning, your mind should be given a short period for rest and integration — say ten minutes — followed by a first review. The second, third, fourth and fifth reviews can take place at increasing intervals, something like a day for the second, a week later for the third, a month later for the fourth, four months later for the fifth.

It is important to remember that reviewing is performed only on the information you really wish to remember, and not on *all* the information you might have taken in while reading the book or listening to a lecture. This ability to select the specific information needed for review can be usefully combined with the ability to extract key words and key areas of

1 Day

1 Week

1 Month

4 Months

When necessary

Review. In order to make sure you do not forget, review needs to be done at the correct time and intervals. The diagram shows a sample review graph for a one-hour learning session. Each review should not take more than five minutes, and the later ones need take only one or two minutes.

meaning. (Techniques for improving this ability are expanded in chapter 6.)

The other advantage of proper reviewing is that the more the information your brain already contains is reviewed, the more easily you will be able to latch on to new, incoming information.

The brain which has forgotten most of what it has learnt will find new learning far more difficult than the brain which is completely up to date, and is ready to compare, contrast, and connect the incoming information with the information already stored.

The situation is reminiscent of the biblical saying: "Unto him that hath shall be given . . . . but from him that hath not shall be taken away even that which he hath." By him that has much knowledge, new knowledge shall more easily be gained; by him that has little knowledge and does not review, new knowledge shall be difficult to acquire, and the little knowledge that he does have will tend to be forgotten.

Special Memory Systems

These memory systems, once described as tricks, are now known to be based on two of the major aspects of memory: linking and outstandingness.

The simple rules for these systems number only two.

1. LINKS. You must make dramatic and simple links between the things you want to remember, or between the things you want to remember and specially prepared memory code lists. This means that you bang things together, place things on top of each other or underneath each other, blend them with each other, or substitute one for the other.

2. OUTSTANDINGNESS. You must exaggerate in every way possible the combined image, using all your senses in the process. This means that the combined image must be much larger than life, garishly coloured, humorous or absurd: and you must, where possible, be able to imagine yourself tasting, touching, hearing, seeing and smelling it.

For example, one of the simplest basic mnemonic

techniques is that known as the link system in which a series of items is simply remembered by applying the two basic rules.

For example, if a man has to 'phone another business man about a contract as soon as he gets into the office; has also to 'phone his wife, and write letters confirming a lunch appointment, adjusting his accounts, and reserving an aeroplane ticket; has to meet a television producer in the afternoon; and has to buy a bottle of wine, peas and paper napkins on the way home, he might remember all this in the following way:

Out of one end of the 'phone, like the genie out of the lamp, he could imagine his business partner emerging and waving the gigantic contract about which they have to talk on the 'phone. From the other end of the 'phone would emerge his wife, juggling with peas and wiping up a broken bottle of wine with paper napkins.

This entire scene he could then imagine as being presented to him on a gigantic television screen.

To remember the three letters—and allowing his imagination really to exaggerate in order to make best use of the mnemonic techniques—he might imagine an enormous lunch on top of the television set, with thousands of pound notes fluttering on to it, dropped from an aeroplane flying overhead.

This example sounds ridiculous, absurd and exaggerated. It is! And the effectiveness of the technique will become clear when you realize that even though this example has nothing to do with you, the reader, you'll have difficulty forgetting it.

A number of people are already using these systems in both home and professional life. Business men, for example, can use such a system to enable them to remember the person they have to call as soon as they get into the office, the significant letters they have to write, the major appointments for the afternoon, and the items they have to pick up from the shops on their way home.

It can also be seen that these systems, once considered "tricks", are soundly based on the way our brains work. They utilize that enormous range of abilities that continually lies dormant in the right brain, waiting only for the opportunity to express itself.

Memory and Observation

It is impossible to remember something your senses have not properly taken in. Memory is consequently largely dependent on the way in which you "allow things in" and this will be dealt with in detail in the following chapters on listening and seeing. Meanwhile, it is appropriate to see how observation can be used to overcome one of the most common of all memory problems: remembering names and faces.

Many people, when introduced to others, "know" that they are going to forget the names anyway and therefore go through a whole series of introductions without looking at one of the faces to whom they are being introduced. Their fear of failure actually guarantees that they do fail. Even those who do look at new faces will often tend to see the "general face" and not really look at its specific characteristics.

Because your recall works by linking and also by outstandingness, it is essential when seeing a new face to look at it properly, so that you can take any opportunity for linking or remembering outstanding features. This does not mean peering rudely at the person's face, but simply taking an active, intelligent interest.

You can prepare your mind for this by "exercising" your observational powers in public places. At different times give yourself different parts of the face to look at, so that on one day you might concentrate on noses, another day on eyebrows, another day on ears, another on general head shapes, etc. You will find to your surprise that each part of each face varies enormously from person to person, and that your increasing observation of the differences will assist you to remember the new faces that you meet.

In order to assist your recall even further you can use linking and review techniques when being introduced. If it is reasonable, ask for the name to be repeated, and then use it politely in the conversation that follows. It is far more considerate of the person you have just met to use his or her name than to refer to "you" or "he" or "she".

In order to establish links, it is often useful to enquire about the derivation of the person's name. This is not impolite, and most people have a fairly deep knowledge of, and interest in, the heritage of their names. During the conversation, if there is anything outstanding about either the face or the name, try to form imaginative links using the same techniques as outlined for the special memory systems.

The pleasant thing about this approach to remembering names and faces is that the more it becomes successful the more confident and open you will become, making the next memory task even more simple.

"Setting" Yourself to Remember

In conjunction with the above it is important to be aware that your memory, if looked after, will continue to improve with age. The work by Rosenzweig, as outlined in the chapter on the brain, emphasized that stimulation increased the number of patterns in the brain. As these memory-loops form what appears to be the bulk of the patterns, it is important to keep the mind stimulated, and to encourage retention and recall practices wherever possible.

This can be done by:

1. Starting a programme of learning new subjects and new languages, in order to increase the basic memory store.

2. Encouraging in yourself any activity that you have noticed helps you to remember.

3. Paying attention to your dreams, checking carefully the memory images which you thought you had "previously forgotten".

4. Occasionally attempting to "take yourself back" to a period in your life, exploring *all* the elements of your life at that time.

5. Keeping a diary using key words, special little drawings, and as many colours as possible.

6. Using the special memory systems and special memory system techniques for pleasure, for exercise, and for remembering.

7. Organizing your learning time so that the primacy and recency effects are maximized, and so that the sag-in-the-middle during learning is minimized.

8. Reviewing, making sure that your review takes place just before the memory of what you want to remember starts to drop.

9. Encouraging the use of your right brain, as it is this side which provides you with the images and colour that make remembering more easy.

10. Trying to see and sense things in as much detail as possible — the more detail you store, the more easy will be your ability to recall.

If you do this, and continue to remind yourself to remember by regularly referring to your books on memory, by leaving reminder notes in appropriate places, by devising review schedules, and by asking other people to do "spot checks" with you, your mind and memory will provide you with increasingly better performance for the rest of your life.

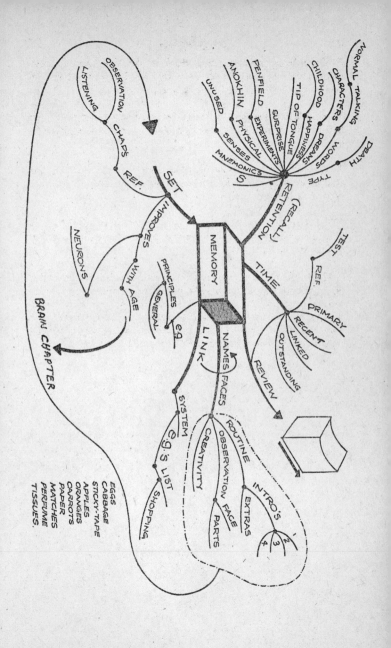

PERSONAL NOTES

3. Listening

Listening is a subject we hear far too little about—one that causes problems for too many people. But there are solutions to many of these problems, solutions which are outlined in this chapter. A special section explains the use of "key" listening, and is followed by a discussion of the relationship of listening to the other senses. As with memory, "setting" for listening is explained.

KEY WORD SUMMARY

> Potential
>
> Problems in concentration
>
> Solutions
>
> Selecting "keys"
>
> Other senses
>
> Setting

The Potential of Your Hearing Ability

Your ear is like the most remarkable musical instrument ever devised. It enables your brain to duplicate the sound of every other instrument, can replay entire symphonies, can select and reject sounds at will, and can communicate all of this perfectly with your brain.

Its capacity is astounding: it can discriminate between millions of different nuances in sound. Between the outer layer of the eardrum and your receiving brain there are tens of thousands of interdependent structures forming the complete unit.

Recent studies of the Mabaans, tribes living near the Sudanese border, have given us fascinating new information about our hearing. The Mabaans are noted for their gentleness of speech and the care they take never to shock their hearing apparatus. These studies showed that all the older members of the Mabaan tribe had hearing just as acute as that of the younger members of the tribe. In other words, there was no natural decline in hearing ability, just as Rosenzweig's studies showed that there was no general decline in mental ability with age.

Hearing, then, like our other abilities, seems to be far more sophisticated than we used to think, as well as being one which, if cared for, does not decline with age. Work by Dr Gerd Jansen and others has also shown that listening plays a very large part in memory, that it is definitely linked to the other brain centres, and that it is one of the essential ingredients of imagination and creativity.

Why is it that our listening habits are so poor, and how can we both improve them and use them to the advantages of memory and our other senses?

Problems in Concentration

Among the main problems experienced in hearing and listening are the following:

1. physical

2. distractions

3. boredom

4. forgetting what was heard

5. indistinct sounds

1. PHYSICAL. Apart from those cases where physical damage is caused by disease, most of the decline in our hearing ability seems to stem from the way we treat our hearing apparatus. It should be treated as a sophisticated musical instrument, which means keeping it in well-tuned running order and not "bashing it about".

In our society we continually bombard our very delicate inner ear with noises that are well above its tolerance level. Where possible it is advisable to avoid close contact with any large machine-generated sounds, especially aeroplanes and

outer ear

eardrum

middle ear

chain of small bones

stirrup
anvil
hammer

semicircular canals

nerves to the brain

cochlea

Your ear is like the most remarkable musical instrument ever devised — it can discriminate between millions of different nuances in sound.

amplifying equipment. As the studies with the Mabaans emphasized, if the ear is looked after no decline need be experienced with age.

2. DISTRACTIONS.
Distractions to listening usually come from two main sources, the environment and our own internal thoughts.

One of the mind's astounding abilities is being able to reject sounds around us in which we are not interested. Thus, at a party, lovers can hear each other's whispered words despite the general havoc around. Similarly, a mother can detect the cry of her child above the shouting of a large crowd.

Simply being aware of this ability will often enable you to eliminate environmental distractions. Rather than concentrating on the noise which is distracting, concentrate on the thing you wish to hear, and the brain will automatically "switch off" the noises you wish not to hear.

Next time you are in a crowded gathering, be conscious of the things that you do hear, and the things that you do not listen to. You will find you are able to pay attention, despite the surrounding noise, to the person in whom you are interested, or to a conversation which contains information that is of importance to you. Notice how your mind and body "set themselves" to listen, and practise using this ability next time you are in a situation where the surrounding noise seems insurmountable. You will often find that it is not insurmountable at all—as shown by the many people who when shouted at or called by name, have reported afterwards that they were so intent on what someone else was saying, they simply did not hear.

In the same way that it can switch off, your brain can also "switch on" its listening abilities. Many people can sleep through the most extraordinary night-time noises, to awaken immediately at the whisper of a loved one or at the sound of a gentle alarm. Once again, knowing this capacity, it is advisable to practise and encourage it—the more it is used, the more it will benefit you.

This you can do by making a conscious decision to listen to any given set of sounds around. If you are on a busy street decide first to listen to the sound of feet on the pavement, then to the sound of voices, then to the sound of car horns, then to the sound of birds, then to the sound of specific types of traffic. Similarly, when you are in your house, listen separately for the different sounds it makes: water sounds, wind sounds, electric sounds, movement sounds.

The second form of distraction results from our own personal thought processes. This can often occur when we are tired, or suffering from undue pressure. One of the most effective ways of eliminating such distractions is to organize the listening/learning situation so that understanding and recall are maximized (see previous chapter, page 42). If this is done, your mind will tend to concentrate on the listening, and not "wander off" because of sagging recall and attention.

All this is very closely associated with another major listening problem:

3. BOREDOM. Boredom usually occurs in a situation where we are "obliged" to pay attention, but in which our interest has not been engaged. The result is usually a fairly immediate wandering of the mind, and an almost total loss of what is being said.

Apart from either leaving or endeavouring to pretend an interest we do not feel, one technique for highly boring situations is strongly recommended: that of the strongly opposed critic.

If you are listening to talk in which you are deeply interested, you will lean forward, "all ears". And this holds good when the speaker is opposed to your own beliefs, or is someone who you particularly wish to argue against.

So lean forward, "all ears", when listening to something boring! Listen with your attention directed to a complete, constructive criticism of all that you are hearing. If you do this, your mind will readily take in all the information you are hearing.

4. FORGETTING. Forgetting what you have been listening to (or should have been listening to) can be embarrassing for you, and signifies a waste of your time as well as of the speaker's. Apart from looking after your hearing apparatus, conquering distractions from the environment and your own mind, and

using the strongly-opposed critic's technique to battle against boredom, there are three more techniques you can use to improve your listening ability:

self-motivation

setting yourself to listen

key selection

Self-motivation is very closely related to will-power and goal-directedness, both of which are among the most tried and tested methods of improving any mental performance.

Setting yourself to listen can be practised by creating your own listening exercises, in which you actively set out to hear more of what goes on around you — at work, while travelling, in conversations, at parties, in the countryside, and while drifting off to sleep. Give yourself little personal tests for detecting the differences between tones of voice, the songs of different birds and the general noise level at your work and home at different times of the day.

Key selection is based on the fact that your mind does not remember in lists, lines and sentences, but by connecting key words and images to each other (see chapter on Note-Making and Fast Writing). To remember what has been said, concentrate not on the general flow of sentences, but on those key elements that are the basis of what is being said. As these key elements gradually build up, try to build a linked pattern of these elements in your mind, visualizing the overall map of ideas as the talk continues. Key selection will not only enable you to recall far more of what you have heard, but will also significantly increase your ability to understand what you are hearing, make appropriate comments and ask intelligent questions.

5. INDISTINCT SOUNDS. This listening problem, of a different order from the others, is most dramatically experienced when trying to follow what another human being is saying. People often miss the main elements of a conversation, lecture or speech, simply because they are reluctant to point out to the speaker that he is *mumbling*. As

the speaker's intention is usually to get his information across, he will more often than not be thankful for a gentle reminder that he cannot be heard properly.

Hearing and Your Other Senses

Research is showing how closely our senses are linked with each other. The previous assumption that the loss of one sense sharpened another is now being questioned. It seems rather that the loss of one sense *forces* us to develop the remaining senses to their maximum, but that the more senses we have, the greater the potential ability of each.

This ability of the senses to support each other is perhaps most dramatically shown by the great memorizers like the Russian "S". "S" continually emphasized in his conversations with the psychologist Aleksandr Luria that whenever he perceived something with any one of his senses, all the other senses automatically joined in and he received a complete sense impression. It was this that enabled him to remember so completely.

Hearing is an especially important sense, and like smell it is one that we have particularly neglected and abused.

Once you make the start in looking after it, you will experience a continuing spiral of progress. No longer will things go in one ear and out the other — they will remain in your brain.

PERSONAL NOTES

4. Using and Caring for Your Eyes

When you consider the quality of vision of the great artist or the amazing co-ordination of hand and eye of the champion tennis player, you begin to glimpse the enormous inherent capacity of your eyes. Here we examine their potential and such interesting questions as *where* you see, *how* you see, or whether you see in the same way as other people. Games and exercises are described which will enable you to discover how your eyes function when they look at moving things, and when they look at still things. The relationship between your vision and your emotions, health, senses and memory is explained and advice is given on ways in which you can develop your analytical observation, expand your visual ability, and use your imagination in order to see more clearly. The final section of the chapter gives exercises for eye care.

KEY WORD SUMMARY

Amazing facts

Where and how?

Eye movement; your movement

Emotions, health, senses and memory

Analytical observation; peripheral vision

Caring for your eyes

pupil

lens

cornea

iris

ciliary muscle

retina

choroid

sclera

eye muscles

optic nerve

Your eye, like your ear, is a miracle of biological engineering. Each of your eyes contains *150 million* separate light receivers.

Your eyes are another miracle of biological engineering. At the back of each there is an area the size of a thumbnail which contains *150 million* separate light receivers. These light receivers can process millions of millions of photons (light energy particles) per second.

As with our brain and the other senses, much general knowledge has now been gathered concerning our eyes, most of it helpful in enabling us to understand and improve the seeing process.

Seeing at the Back of Your Head

Paradoxically we see at the back of our heads. A large area at the back of our brain called the occipital lobe processes all the information our eyes send to it via the optic nerve. This is one reason why it is particularly dangerous to hit someone in the back of the head, such a blow having been known to cause instant and permanent blindness.

Pupil Size

We have known for some time that pupil size adjusts according to light intensity and nearness. The brighter the light and the nearer the object, the smaller will the pupil size be.

Western scientists have recently discovered that pupil size also varies with emotion, and that if you are confronted with a sight that especially interests you (like a member of the opposite sex) your pupil size will automatically increase. Such changes are small, but can be noticed by careful observation. Jade dealers in China have been aware of it for many years. While presenting objects for the customer's inspection, the dealer pays particularly close attention to the customer's eyes, waiting for an increase in pupil size. When this increase has been observed, the dealer knows that the customer is "hooked" and sets an appropriate price.

Do You See as Others See?

A question which has intrigued thinkers and philosophers for centuries is whether one person sees the same thing as another. If I see a colour and call it "red" and you see the same colour and agree that it is indeed "red", we still cannot be certain that we are seeing "the same thing". For both you and I have been trained to call that light vibration, whenever we see it, "red"; but we do not know whether the same light vibration gives each of us an identical *internal* image.

In different moods the same things will be experienced as quite different. Witness the lovers who see everything through "rose-tinted spectacles", and the depressed person who sees everything as "black".

Eye Movement

Before reading on, perform this little exercise: Look straight ahead of you, and imagine that an ordinary paperback book is being held up for you to read about one foot from your eyes. With your forefinger trace the speed and movement at which your eyes normally read. Do this now.

Most people move their finger in a smooth regular line, swinging from the end of one line to the beginning of another, much like the motion of a typewriter.

This idea of a smooth flowing motion is wrong, because our eyes can normally focus clearly on something only if they are still in relation to that object. If the object is still, the eyes must be almost still. If the object is moving, the eyes must move with it.

To demonstrate this to yourself, try the following exercise: First hold the tip of your forefinger still in front of you, and focus on it intently, noticing what your eyes are doing. Next move the tip of the forefinger around, up and down and in zigzags, going to the very edge of your vision, all the while watching the tip *intently* with both of your eyes (see fig., p. 69).

You will have noticed that when your finger was still your eyes remained perfectly still, and that when your fingertip moved, your eyes moved with it, tracking it continuously.

Now try another exercise: Put both hands up to the side of your head as if you are the victim of a hold-up. Smoothly and simultaneously, move them across your face so that your arms

make an X in front of you, then smoothly move them back to
the original hold-up position. Throughout the exercise visually
follow each hand *individually*. As you perform the exercise,
again notice your eyes' behaviour throughout.

In that exercise you will have noticed that it was impossible
to follow both hands at the same time, unless you are one of
those rare people who can swivel their eyes independently.

These exercises serve to emphasize that our eyes need to
"fix" on something if they are to see it clearly, in much the
same way as a camera needs to be "held" on the object of the
picture. For example, in order to take a picture of a moving
car, the camera must move *with* the car. The resulting image
of the car will be very clear, but will have a background that is
completely blurred. This knowledge becomes especially
significant in fast reading, as the next chapter will show.

It is also useful in various day-to-day situations. For
example, many people in trains have great difficulty seeing the
names on stations they are passing through, not because their
eyes are unable to see, but because they don't use them
properly. If they aimed their eyes on the name as it first
appeared, and "fixed" on it as it went past, they would have a
complete second in which their eyes held it still for them to
read. This is better than vaguely looking out of the window
and getting an impression of blurs as the train speeds through.

The Relationship of Vision to Health, Emotions, Other Senses and Memory

1. HEALTH. More often than not, a healthy body provides
healthy vision. This, of course, means regular exercise,
adequate sleep, and a well-balanced diet. If you think back,
you will probably be able to recall that when for any reason
you had no exercise at all for a period, both your body and
vision became sluggish; that when you were not getting
enough sleep, your eyes rapidly became red and "bleary"; and
that when your diet was unbalanced, especially if laced too
liberally with alcohol, your vision not only became blurred,
but may even have disappeared momentarily altogether!

2. EMOTIONS. Eye specialists have noticed with increasing
frequency, that many eye problems are not physical in origin,

This exercise shows you how your eyes work when they are focusing their attention on a moving object.

but are the result of boredom or tension. Eyes which are continually bored "go slack" and will either receive blurred images, or will tend not to focus at all.

Similarly tension has a negative effect on vision, forcing the eyes into a more rigid and strained observation pattern, resulting in unclear vision.

People in a state of dynamic relaxation or special alertness often report exceptionally clear vision. This is supported by the commonsense observation that very happy people's eyes seem to "sparkle", the simple reflection of good visual health.

3. THE OTHER SENSES. Vision, like hearing, is intricately linked with all the other senses. The more extensively it is used, the "sharper" the other senses become. This close working harmony of the senses can be easily recognized if you remember the disturbance caused to your perception whenever sound and vision become unsynchronized on film or television.

4. MEMORY. Vision is one of our most powerful sources of memory. The importance of correct observation becomes clear when we realize that our memory store is based on the information fed into it. If the eyes are letting through blurred images, the memory will not be able to operate as clearly or as accurately as it should. The relationship is almost direct: the more clearly and accurately we observe, the more clearly and more accurately will we remember.

Once again the perfect memory man, the Russian "S", made some relevant comments. He explained that when he was remembering something, he would often close his eyes and "re-see" the thing he had originally been observing. His original observation was therefore essential to his perfect memory. This habit of closing the eyes to remember something is not uncommon, and you often see people, when racking their brains for a visual memory, closing their eyes in order to see it more clearly.

In view of all this new information, it is now possible to recommend a series of exercises for expanding your observational abilities, and for taking special care of your eyes.

Hold both hands to the side of your head, and then move them evenly and smoothly back and forward in front of your face, looking at *each* hand clearly as they pass back and forward. This exercise will show you basic facts about how your eyes see.

71

Exercises in Observation

1. ANALYTICAL. When a baby is first born, all he can see is a great blur of confused shades of light. During his first few weeks, the brain sets about decoding the environment — "figuring out" what the various relationships are. This the brain does by storing the important pieces of information, and then continually checking them until the relationship of the object with its environment is clearly established. In this way the child rapidly learns to distinguish the difference between furniture and living beings, as well as the different functions for things, such as containing, pouring, and cutting. Once the basic distinctions have been made, the brain will often tend to take a rest, satisfied that all its labels are appropriate.

If the brain is left in this state, it will tend to become rigid and inflexible, learning little as the years progress, and developing bad recall habits, as exemplified by people who cannot remember names and faces, simply because they have labelled them all as "faces" without observing the distinctions.

The next and natural stage following the labelling, is to look more closely at the make-up of the object labelled. This rapidly heightens general awareness, as well as indicating that among the "same" objects there are an almost infinite number of variations. In order to develop this natural ability, it is necessary to exercise analytical observation. In fact, most readers will have exercised it in areas of their speciality, the artist having developed a special "eye" for art, the naturalist being able to pick out different animals, birds and plants at a glance, and a surveyor being able to determine various structural aspects of buildings. What is essential is that this ability should be developed in all aspects.

The exercise is as follows:

"Set" your mind, at different times and on different days, microscopically to observe different aspects of your surroundings. The kinds of things you can concentrate on are: horizons, the colour of clothes, the differing shapes of plants, the posture and movement of people, and the varying shades and shapes of clouds in the sky, and so on. In each of these exercises it is important to shift your focus continually,

Knowing how your eyes work can enable you to see things
most people do not see.

registering as many different parts of the complete object as you can.

A useful addition to this exercise is to practise analytical observation, and then to close your eyes and try to see completely in your mind's eye the object you have just observed. Next, open your eyes, check the real thing with your mental image, and close your eyes again, making any necessary corrections. Repeat this until the observed image and the mental image are identical.

This second part of the exercise not only increases your observational abilities, but immensely improves both memory and creativity, by giving your brain a much larger and clearer store of images to draw from and to use in the making of new creative images.

2. PERIPHERAL. Supplementing your normal sharp focus vision is an enormous and relatively unexplored area of vision known as peripheral vision. Of the 150 million light receivers in the retina, only a small proportion (just under 5%) lie in the region that is used for acute vision. The remainder are devoted to your peripheral vision.

This is the vision which prevents you from knocking things over, and which guides you during many of your movements. It is often called "unconscious" vision. "Super-conscious" would be a more appropriate term, for its accuracy and efficiency are truly remarkable.

Perhipheral vision also helps you to be "on the look-out" for things. If you have just bought a different model car, when you go for your first drive you will notice on the road other cars of the same model — regardless of whether they are directly in front of you or partially concealed in side roads. Similarly, anyone with a temporary or permanent obsession will continually pick out those items in the environment which relate to him.

This ability does not much depend on ordinary focusing, for often the things picked out are at the edge of the field of vision.

To increase this ability, practise "looking out of the sides of your eyes" while keeping them focused straight ahead. When you are sitting still, whether it be in your office or in a room at

Peripheral vision. Your eyes see more than just straight ahead. Practise using your peripheral vision and you will improve your general mental performance.

home, look straight ahead, focusing clearly on an object in front of you. Maintaining this fixed focus, look around the room, not in the way your normally do but with your "inner eye", seeing how clearly you can distinguish things far to the left, far to the right, above you and below you.

When you are a passenger (not the driver!) in a moving vehicle, similarly look straight ahead, paying special attention to all that is passing by at the *very edges* of your field of vision. This will include hedges, trees, houses and other cars.

Peripheral vision is especially strong at night time, because the numerous light receivers devoted to peripheral vision are sensitive to lower amounts of light than the sharp-focus receivers. Therefore, if you wish to see more clearly in the dark, don't look straight at the object you wish to see, for you will be focusing the wrong part of your eye on it. Practise looking at it from an angle of approximately 30 degrees and you will see it far more clearly.

The next chapter explains how techniques of observation can be applied to reading and to learning.

Caring for Your Eyes

You may find the following brief exercises useful for general eye care:

1. BLINKING. Most people "go tense" when paying special attention, or when reading. As a result they tend to stare, neglecting to blink. This causes eye strain and prevents the necessary lubrication and circulation of blood to the eyes. Therefore, when you are concentrating on something, make sure that you continue to blink while you concentrate, as well as occasionally looking away and simply blinking while you rest your eyes.

2. PALMING. Whenever your eyes are doing a reasonable amount of work, give them regular small rests by closing your eyes and cupping them in your hands. The hand should not touch the eye but simply form a little dome over it. During this rest period it is useful to imagine pure black, as this also gives the mind a rest from visual processing.

3. BREATHING. As with blinking, breathing tends to be "held" whenever we concentrate. This automatically causes tensions in other parts of the body and vision is one of the areas that suffers. Therefore, whenever you are involved in long periods of concentration, try to make sure that your breathing is relaxed and regular. The benefits to your sight will be enormous.

4. FOR PEOPLE WITH GLASSES. The exercises in this and the next chapter apply to all people, whether or not they have glasses. Some have found that after doing the recommended exercises, they have been able to change to glasses one strength less than those they were wearing, because the relaxation of eye tension enables the eye to start to regain a positive process back towards its more natural state. Further gains can be made by ensuring that your glasses are always clean; by becoming conscious of the fact that it is often possible to improve faulty eyesight; by visiting a specialist who emphasizes your eyes rather than your glasses; and by reading Aldous Huxley's *The Art of Seeing*.

5. LIGHT. Daylight is always the best light for observation. Of the artificial lights fluorescent is the worst, for it throws virtually no shadows. This tends to eliminate contrast, which is a vital part of seeing.

Each of these caring techniques, like the exercises, will assist both general vision and reading in particular — see the next chapter.

PERSONAL NOTES

5. Speed Reading and Effective Reading

Why is the history of speed reading so controversial, and what are the reasons for the failure of certain speed reading schools? This chapter answers these questions. The way your eye works and moves while reading is then explained and diagrammed, and special exercises help you to find out how your own eyes function as they read. New techniques are described for high-speed reading with the use of a guide. A special section outlines a complete method for handling reference, technical and study reading. Finally, additional hints are given for "topping up" your reading speed and efficiency.

KEY WORD SUMMARY

> History
>
> Eye movement
>
> Visual guiding
>
> Study reading
>
> Useful hints

Speed Reading Test

Read at your normal pace the following passage on memory by the author. Then calculate your reading speed in words per minute. The total number of words in the passage is approximately 1,300. Check the time as you start to read, and check it again as you finish; then divide 1,300 by the number of minutes you took to read the passage. This will give you your reading speed.

THE HISTORY OF MEMORY

From the time when man first began to depend on his mind for coping with the environment, the possession of an excellent memory has placed individuals in positions of both command and respect. The amazing feats in remembering accomplished by particular people were so impressive that they have become legendary.

THE GREEKS. It is difficult to say exactly when and where the first integrated ideas on memory arose. It is reasonable to state, however, that the first sophisticated concepts can be attributed to the Greeks some 600 years before the birth of Christ.

As we look back on them now, these "sophisticated" ideas were surprisingly naive, especially since some of the men proposing them are numbered among the greatest thinkers the world has ever known.

In the 6th century B.C., Parmenides thought of memory as being a mixture of light and dark or heat and cold. He thought that as long as any given mixture remained unstirred, the memory would be perfect. As soon as the mixture was altered, forgetting occurred.

In the 5th century B.C. Diogenes of Apollonia advanced a different theory. He suggested that memory was a process which consisted of events producing an equal distribution of air in the body. Like Parmenides he thought that when this equilibrium was disturbed forgetting would occur.

Not surprisingly, the first person to introduce a really major idea in the field of memory was Plato, in the 4th century B.C. His theory is known as the Wax Tablet hypothesis and is still accepted by some people today, although there is growing disagreement. To Plato the mind accepted impressions in the same way that wax becomes marked when a pointed object is moved around on its surface. Once the impression had been made, Plato assumed it remained until with time it wore away, leaving a smooth surface once more. This smooth surface was, of course, what Plato considered to be complete forgetting—the opposite aspect of the same process. As will become clear later, many people now feel that they are actually two quite different processes.

Shortly after Plato, Zeno the Stoic slightly modified Plato's ideas, suggesting that sensations actually "wrote" impressions on the wax tablet. When Zeno referred to the mind and its memory he did not place it in any particular organ or section of the body: "mind" was a loose and very unclear concept. The first man to introduce a more scientific terminology was Aristotle, in the late 4th century B.C. He maintained that the language previously used was not adequate to explain the physical aspects of memory. In applying his new language Aristotle attributed to the heart most of the functions that we properly attribute to the brain. Part of the heart's function, he realized, was concerned with the blood, and he felt that memory was based on the blood's movements. He thought forgetting to be the result of a gradual slowing down of these movements.

Aristotle made another important contribution to subsequent thinking on the subject of memory when he introduced his laws of the association of ideas. The concept of association of ideas and images is now generally thought to be of major importance to memory.

In the 3rd century B.C. Herophilus introduced to the discussion "vital" and "animal" spirits. He considered the higher order spirits produced the lower order animal spirits, which included the memory, the brain, and the nervous system. All of these he thought to be secondary in importance to the heart.

It is interesting to note that one reason advanced by Herophilus for man's superiority over animals was the large number of creases in man's brain. (These creases are now known as convolutions of the cortex.) Despite the *fact* of his observation, Herophilus offered no *reason* for his conclusion. It was not until the 19th century, over 2,000 years later, that the real importance of the cortex was discovered.

In summary, the Greeks made the following significant contribution: they were the first to seek a physical as opposed to a spiritual basis for memory; they developed scientific concepts and a language structure that helped the development of these concepts; and they contributed the Wax Tablet hypothesis which suggested that memory and forgetting were opposite aspects of the same process.

THE ROMANS. Surprisingly, the contributions of the Romans were minimal. The major thinkers of their time, including Cicero in the 1st century B.C. and Quintilian in the 1st century A.D., accepted without question the Wax Tablet concept of memory, and did little further work.

Their major contribution was in the development of memory systems. It was they who first introduced the idea of a Link system and a Room system.

THE INFLUENCE OF THE CHRISTIAN CHURCH. The next major contributor to the progress of ideas on memory was the great physician Galen in the 2nd century A.D. He located and delineated various anatomical and physiological structures, as well as further investigating the function and structure of the nervous system.

Like the later Greeks, he assumed that memory and mental processes were part of the lower order of animal spirits. These spirits he thought were manufactured in the sides of the brain, and it was consequently here that memory was seated.

Galen thought that air was sucked into the brain, mixing with the vital spirits. This mixture produced animal spirits which were pushed down through the nervous system, enabling us to feel and taste, etc.

Galen's ideas on memory were rapidly accepted and condoned by the Church which at this time was beginning to exert a great influence. His ideas became doctrine, and on that account little progress was made in the field for 1,500 years. This mental suppression stifled some of the greatest minds that philosophy and science has produced.

St. Augustine in the 4th century A.D. accepted the Church's ideas, considering memory to be a function of the soul, which had a physical seat in the brain. He never expanded on the anatomical aspects of his ideas.

From the time of St. Augustine until the 17th century there were virtually no significant developments in ideas on memory, and even in the 17th century new ideas were restricted by doctrine.

Even such great a thinker as Descartes accepted Galen's basic ideas, although he thought that animal spirits were sent from the pineal gland on special courses through the brain until they came to the part where memory could be triggered. The more clear-cut these courses, the more readily, he thought, would they open when animal spirits travelled through them. It was in this way that he explained the improvement of memory and the development of what are known as "memory traces". A memory trace is a physical change in the nervous system that was not present before learning. The trace enables us to recall.

Another great philosopher, who "went along with the tide" was Thomas Hobbes, who discussed and considered the idea of memory but had little to add to what had been said before. He agreed with Aristotle's ideas, rejecting non-physical explanations of memory. He did not, however, specify the real nature of memory, nor did he make any significant attempts to locate it accurately.

In summary, it is evident from the theories of the 16th century intellectuals that the influence of Galen and the Church had been profound. Almost without exception these great thinkers uncritically accepted primitive ideas on memory.

Now that you have completed the reading, make your best recall notes on the passage you have just read. When you are making the notes, do not refer back to the text.

The "average" score in such passages is a reading speed of about 100 to 300 words a minute, with a comprehension score of between 40% and 70%. The trained reader can often reach speeds well above 600 words per minute, with virtually full comprehension. The ways in which this can be accomplished are outlined in this chapter.

When people make their "best recall notes" they often write them in the form of sentences or long phrases. The more advanced note-makers will concentrate their efforts on key phrases, and the exceptionally advanced will have concentrated their efforts in "key words". There are now new note-making techniques which go beyond even the best of these traditional note-making methods. (These new techniques are explained, with details and exercises for practice, in the chapter on Note-Making and Fast Writing.)

The History of Speed Reading

Although speed reading can be traced to the beginning of this century, when the publication explosion swamped readers with more than they could possibly handle at normal reading rates, most early courses and information were based on information provided from a rather unexpected source; the air force.

Air force tacticians had noticed that a number of pilots were unable to distinguish, when flying, planes seen at a distance. In the life and death situation of combat, this inability was obviously an enormous disadvantage, and the air force psychologists and educationalists set about to remedy the situation. They developed a machine called a tachistoscope, which is simply a device for flashing images for varying instants of time on a large screen. They started by flashing fairly large pictures of friendly and enemy aircraft at very slow exposures and then gradually shortened the exposure while decreasing the size of the image seen. They found to their surprise that, with training, the average person was able to distinguish almost speck-like representations of different planes when the images had been flashed on the screen for only 1/500th of a second.

Reasoning that the perceptual ability of the eyes had been vastly underrated, they decided to transfer this information to reading. Using exactly the same device and process, they first flashed one large word for as long as 5 seconds on a screen, gradually reducing the size of the word and shortening the length of the flash. This they were able to do until they were flashing four words simultaneously on a screen for 1/500th of a second, and were still able to obtain recognition.

As a consequence of this approach, most speed reading courses and kits were based on tachistoscopic training.

This approach usually provided the student with a graph graded in units of 10 from 100 to 400 words per minute (see figure, p.87). Most people, with regular training, were able to climb from an average of 200 per minute to an average of 400 per minute (also shown in figure, p. 87). Unfortunately, the graduates of such training schemes reported a general dissatisfaction after a few weeks of "postgraduate reading". An enormous number of them noticed that shortly after the course had finished, their reading speed once again sank to their previous level.

Only recently was it realized that the *normal range* of reading ability is from between roughly 200 to 400 words per minute and that most people operate at the lowest level of this range. The increasing reading· ability observed in the tachistoscopic courses had in fact little to do with the tachistoscopic training, but was more a function of motivation being eked out over a period of weeks and of the readers' reaching the top of their normal range. Another explanation for the failure of the still screen approach can be found by referring back to the basic rule of observation: In order to see something clearly, the eye must be still in relation to the object it is seeing.

Basic Eye Movements

Because the words on the page are still, the eye must be still when it is looking at them, but because there are many words to read, the eye must also *move*. This apparently paradoxical situation, in which the eye is required both to be still and to move, is resolved by putting the two in sequence: The eye must be still to take in a single word or group of words, and then

A

400
350
300
250
200
150
100

individual
progress,
tachistoscope
trained

B

1000
900
800
700
600
500
400
300
200
100

individual progress
properly trained

average progress
tachistoscope
trained

Traditionally, speed-reading schools gave their students graphs like A which
were graded from 100 to 400. A small improvement therefore looked large.
Reading ability should be measured on graphs reaching a maximum of
1,000 or more words a minute, like B. The improvement with tachistoscope
training is small in comparison to what can be achieved with more efficient
methods.

must move to the next group of words where it must again be
still, before moving on to the next word or group of words, and
so on. The eye must therefore *primarily* be trained, not to see
flashes, but to *move* efficiently.

The eye movements of the slow reader, complete with back-
skipping, regression, and visual wandering off the page are
shown in the top diagram opposite. The lower diagram shows
the eye movement of the more efficient reader, without back-
skipping, regression and wandering, and with a larger number
of words taken in for each "stop", or fixation.

In order to see how these movements and stops work, try the
following exercise. Work with a partner, holding an open
book in front of you just above eye level. First read a few lines
exceptionally slowly, stopping on every word or syllable. Next
read a few lines exceptionally fast, taking in as large "chunks"
as you possibly can. While you perform this exercise your
partner will watch the way your eyes move, and then describe
the performance to you when you have finished the exercise.
Once this has been completed, reverse roles so that you can
see, from your partner's performance, how the eyes actually
move while reading.

You will notice that the faster reader moves his eyes
smoothly across the page with regular stops on larger groups of
words. This further helps to explain why the tachistoscopic
training methods were relatively unsuccessful. Rather than
concentrating on the movement and flow of eye fixations, they
held the eyes still throughout the training, thus eliminating
the major factor in faster and more effective reading.

If you wish to improve your reading speed, you can dispose
of the various tachistoscope methods, and concentrate on
motivating yourself to read faster, taking two or more words
per fixation, and making sure that your eye moves in an even
flow, with as few regressions, back-skippings and wanderings
as possible.

There is another technique you can use which is especially
helpful:

Using a Visual Guide

If you have ever watched children learning to read, you will
have noticed that they invariably point to the word on which

These illustrations show how poor readers read one word at a time, their eyes stopping on each word and then moving on to the next, with back-skipping and wandering-off-the-page; how advanced or efficient readers take in three or more words at every visual stop. Advanced readers will have reduced their back-skipping and wandering-off-the-page to a minimum. Their comprehension and understanding will also be greater.

they are momentarily concentrating. They do this because the
pointer gives them an accurate reference, as well as preventing
the eyes from wandering and back-skipping. We tell them to
take their finger off the page because we feel that it slows them
down, but this is not in fact the case. You can easily
demonstrate this by counting off 200 words on a page, and by
guiding your eyes along them with your finger so that you
cover the complete 200 in exactly 1 minute. You will find the
guide revealing to you the uncomfortable truth that 200 words
per minute is, to look at, an incredibly slow speed; your finger
and eye will probably both feel held back; they both want to
go faster.

Accountants can also be seen using a visual guide when
adding up large columns of numbers. Rather than simply
"reading them off", they will guide their eye down the side of
the columns with a pen or pencil. This guiding helps them to
keep their place, and at the same time improves the visual flow
and increases concentration.

A number of studies have recently shown that the use of a
visual guide will increase reading speed by as much as 100%,
while also improving comprehension, understanding and
memory. The guide focuses attention, encourages the eye to
keep moving in a smooth and rhythmical fashion, and
discourages the bad habits of regression, back-skipping and
visual wandering.

It is a far more useful reading device than a card moved
down the page under each line, because the visual guide
emphasizes the horizontal movement of reading, whereas the
card only identifies one whole line. The print below the words
being read is moreover left clear for the peripheral vision to
get a preview of what is coming.

The most effective way of using a visual guide is to point it
just beneath the words you are reading, keeping its movement
smooth and regular so that your eyes can pick out, as they
choose, the appropriate groups of words.

The visual guide can also be used as a speed training device.
If you want to continue to improve your speed, give yourself
frequent training sessions in which you move the guide a little
faster than is comfortable for adequate comprehension. If you
can maintain this faster speed, you will find that your brain,

A visual guide improves reading efficiency. The guide should be long and thin like a pencil, and should be moved smoothly along *underneath* the line being read. The guide can either be resting on the page or held slightly above it.

rather than giving up, will increase its concentration and begin to comprehend at the new and faster speed.

It is also worth occasionally trying super-speed training, in which you move the guide as fast as your hand can possibly move across the page, taking in with your eyes whatever odd glimpses you can. This training accustoms your eye to move exceptionally fast across print, and encourages it to establish new and higher "norms" for reading speed.

Reference, Technical and Study Reading

Before getting down to the business of actually reading, it is essential to prepare yourself properly for the task. This preparation involves four major steps:

1. time

2. amount

3. knowledge

4. aims and goals

1. TIME. In the chapter on Memory you saw how understanding, comprehension and recall are vastly improved if your time is organized into reasonable learning units. This is especially important at the beginning of technical reading, for not only does it enable you to maximize recall and learning, it also enables you to make more sensible judgements about the amount you will be able to cover in the time period.

2. AMOUNT. Next, it is important to make a reasonable estimate of the amount to be covered in the time you have given yourself. While making this estimate, you should also break up the amount into reasonable units, corresponding with the units of time you have planned for yourself.

Pre-planning the time and amount in this way gives you the psychological advantage of "knowing where you are going" rather than meandering off into a threatening and unknown territory, with no particular goal in sight.

3. KNOWLEDGE. In order to "tune up" your mind, it is advisable to do a brief review (2 to 5 minutes) of any knowledge you already have which is relevant to what you are about to read. This establishes all the right connections in your brain, and makes it far more easy for you to "latch on" to the new information that will be coming in. This can be especially important when reading up-to-date journals and papers, etc.

If the material you are reading is totally new, it is often advisable to go first to a reference book, such as an encyclopaedia. This will give you an introductory overview of any new subject, giving your mind the necessary and basic hooks it needs to grapple with the new information.

4. AIMS AND GOALS. By setting yourself reasonable aims and goals, you can further "tune up" your mind for the task ahead. Jot down the questions you want answered from whatever you are about to read, and then read actively for the answers. You will find that if you have asked the right questions, even new material will seem somehow familiar, and your learning will be much easier.

The questions you set yourself, apart from being specifically directed to the aim you have in mind, should also include some that are as open-minded and as open-ended as possible. This open-minded and open-ended approach will help you to absorb new information and to avoid reading only what you want to read—an easily acquired habit of mind that tends towards a "funnel vision" approach to learning.

If you have difficulty in establishing your aims and goals, you can always start with those questions that children ask of their parents:

> how
>
> when
>
> where
>
> why
>
> what
>
> who
>
> definitions

This series of questions, which I often call the "kids' kit", covers most of the important areas in any subject; for example: "when" picks out all items of historical importance, "who" hooks on to all the major people, and so on.

After having organized your time limit, chosen the amount and divided it into reasonable sections, and tuned up your mind by reviewing your present knowledge and establishing aims and goals, you are now more than prepared.

Applying Yourself to the Reading Task

At this stage, most people start "ploughing through" from the first page, which is definitely not the most efficient way to read. A better way is similar to that in which most people approach jigsaw puzzles.

Usually, people look at the picture on the box first, and find out how many pieces there are in the entire puzzle. They then find a suitable place in which to do the puzzle, open the box, tip out the pieces and turn them all right-side up. They follow this by sorting out the edge and corner pieces and then arranging the pieces by general colour areas. They select special areas, and begin to fill in. When coming across difficult pieces, they put them aside, waiting for a later stage when they will more easily fit them in.

The jigsaw approach can be most usefully applied to the reading of technical references, trade journals, management books, learned papers, and study texts, and should normally involve the following stages:-

1. survey

2. preview

3. inview

4. review

1. SURVEY. The purpose of the survey is to give you an outline of the material you are about to read. Check first to see if there is any summary or conclusion. If there is, read it first, for it

gives you the kernel of what you are about to read. During the survey you should also cover, if they exist, the following items:

> table of contents
>
> photographs
>
> graphs
>
> number tables
>
> marginal comments
>
> footnotes
>
> chapter headings
>
> sub-headings
>
> glossaries
>
> index

When you have finished this stage you will usually be able to decide whether you wish to read in greater depth. If you do, move on to the next stage.

2. PREVIEW. The preview is similar to the survey, except that it is done on the text itself. When previewing, it is usually advisable to check the beginnings and ends of chapters, sections and paragraphs. Many authors condense much of their information in these areas, and it is a quick and efficient way of further checking the general outline of a book.

During this stage you should place visible markers at the division points which mark your time periods, and in pages to which you may need to refer continually.

The preview, like the survey, might prove to be the last stage of your reading, especially if you find the material does not meet with your aims and goals, is of a level too difficult for you, or has already answered your questions.

3. INVIEW. The inview can be compared to the stage where you begin to fill in the jigsaw puzzle. During this stage you will normally be rooting more deeply for answers to your questions, and should be marking with a soft pencil on the

margin those areas to which you wish to return, either because they are especially noteworthy or because they present you with momentary difficulty. *Do not* at this stage worry over difficulties. Leave them, as with the jigsaw puzzle, until the end.

4. REVIEW. This is your final stage, and at this point in your reading you should be checking that your aims and goals have been generally accomplished, reviewing what you have read, making final notes (for methods of making notes, see the next chapter) and planning your on-going review and next study period.

It is important to realize that this approach is, above all things, *flexible*. A very difficult mathematics or physics book might require two or three surveys, and two or three reviews. A light novel might require simply one skimmed reading. The book on which you wish to write a special paper or report might require a number of inviews, each with a different aim or goal in mind. Your technical journal might require a flip through or an in-depth study.

If you begin to approach reading in this way, you will find to your surprise and enjoyment that it becomes increasingly easy. The more you learn, the easier it will be to take in new knowledge, which means an automatic increase in reading speed. The increase in speed means that even more knowledge will be acquired and the positive spiral has begun.

Useful Hints

In addition to this general approach, there are a number of other useful things you can do to help you with your general reading:

1. SPEED. Before any reading do a quick "dash" over the print. This will both briefly accustom your eyes to higher speeds, and will ensure that they are "warmed up" for the reading task ahead.

2. TEMPERATURE. For learning it is always best to have a slightly cool rather than a slightly warm temperature. 16–18°C (68–70°F) is ideal.

3. SURROUNDINGS. Make sure that your surroundings are pleasant — but not *too* comfortable! Your learning area should preferably be free of anything which could distract you while you are reading.

4. EYE REST. During extended reading periods, make sure that you regularly look up from the book and focus on distant objects. This relaxes and rests the muscles of the eye, enabling you to carry on reading without unnecessary fatigue.

5. VISUALIZING. Occasionally stop, close your eyes, and try to reproduce, in your mind's eye, a page of print, a photograph or graph that you have just looked at. Apart from providing a useful rest, this will significantly help to increase your recall, while providing useful training for your imagination.

6. POSTURE. Your posture should be reasonably upright, but not rigid or tense. If it is correct, and if your desk or table surface is at a reasonable height, the distance between your eyes and book should be between 15 and 24 inches.

These techniques can be supplemented with exercises outlined in the previous chapter. If you practise them regularly, your reading will become a far more enjoyable and much less tense experience.

Check Yourself Again

When you have finished the *entire book*, return to this continuation of the essay on memory that you began earlier in this chapter, time yourself again and calculate your words per minute (there are 1,300 words in this passage also). Afterwards make your best recall notes in key words and patterns. (The key word and pattern approach is explained in the following chapter.) When you have completed this entire exercise, compare both results with your speed of reading and note-making in the initial reading exercise.

THE HISTORY OF MEMORY — continued

TRANSITIONAL PERIOD — THE 18TH CENTURY. One of the first thinkers to be influenced by the new surge of science and by the ideas of Newton was David Hartley, who developed the vibratory theory of memory. Applying Newton's ideas on vibrating particles, Hartley suggested that there were memory vibrations in the brain which began before birth. New sensations modified existing vibrations in degree, kind, place and direction. After influence by a new sensation, vibrations quickly returned to their natural state. But if the same sensation appeared again the vibrations took a little longer to return. This progression would finally result in the vibrations remaining in their "new" state, and a memory trace was established.

Other major thinkers of this period included Zanotti who was the first to link electrical forces with brain functions, and Charles Bonnet who developed the ideas of Hartley in relation to the flexibility of nerve fibres. The more often nerves were used, the more easily he thought they vibrated, and the better memory would then be.

The theories of these men were more sophisticated than previous ones because they had been largely influenced by developments in related scientific fields. This interaction of ideas laid the groundwork for some of the more modern theories of memory in the 19th century.

THE 19TH CENTURY. With the progress of science in Germany in the 19th century, some important developments occurred. Many of the ideas initiated by the Greeks were overthrown, and work on memory expanded to include the biological sciences.

Prochaska finally and irrevocably rejected the age-old idea of animal spirits, on the ground that it has no scientific basis and no evidence to support it. He felt that limited existing knowledge made speculation on the location of memory in the brain a waste of time. "Spatial localization may be possible," he said, "but we just do not know enough at the moment to make it a useful idea." It was not for fifty years that localizing the area of memory became a useful pursuit.

Another major theory presented in this century was that of Marie-Jean-Pierre Flourens, who "located" the memory in *every* part of the brain. He said that the brain acted as a whole and could not be interpreted as an interaction of elementary parts. His views held the field of physiology for some time, and it is only recently that great strides have been made in the development of our thinking on memory.

MODERN THEORIES. Modern developments in memory have been aided to an enormous degree by advances in technology and methodology. Almost without exception psychologists and other thinkers in this field agree that memory is located in the cortex, which is the large area of the brain covering the surface of the cerebrum. Even today however, the exact localization of memory areas is proving a difficult task, as is the accurate understanding of the function of memory itself.

Current thought has progressed from Hermann Ebbinghaus's work with learning and forgetting curves at the turn of the century, to advanced and complex theories.

Research and theory can be roughly divided into three main areas: work on establishing a biochemical basis for memory; theories which suggest that memory can no longer be considered as a single process but must be broken down into divisions; and Wilder Penfield's work on brain stimulation.

Research into the biochemical basis for memory was initiated by Hyden in the late 1950s. This theory suggests that RNA (ribonucleic acid), a complex molecule, serves as a chemical mediator for memory.

RNA is produced by the substance DNA (deoxyribonucleic acid) which is responsible for our genetic inheritance—for example DNA decides whether your eyes will be blue or brown.

A number of experiments have been performed with RNA, lending support to the idea that it does indeed have a lot to do with the way in which we remember things. For example, if animals are given certain types of training, the RNA found in certain cells is changed. And further, if the production of

RNA in an animal's body is stopped or modified, these animals are unable to learn or remember.

An even more exciting experiment showed that when RNA was taken from one rat and injected into another, the second rat "remembered" things that he had never been taught, but which the first rat had.

While research into this aspect of memory is progressing, other theorists are saying that we should stop emphasizing "memory" and concentrate more on the study of "forgetting". It is their position that we do not so much remember as gradually forget.

Encompassing this idea is the duplex theory of remembering and forgetting which states that there are two different kinds of information retention: long-term and short-term. For example, you have probably experienced a different "feeling" in the way you recall a telephone number which has just been given to you, and the way you recall your own telephone number.

The short-term situation is one in which the idea is "in" the brain but has not yet been properly coded and is therefore more readily forgotten. In the long-term situation the idea has been completely coded, filed and stored and will probably remain for years, if not for life.

Research into direct brain stimulation was initiated by Dr Wilder Penfield, a clinical surgeon. When performing craniotomies (removal of a small section of the brain) in order to reduce epileptic attacks, Penfield had first to remove a portion of the skull lying over the side of the brain. Before operating Penfield conducted a systematic electrical stimulation of the open brain, and the patient, who remained conscious, reported his experience after each stimulation. In an early case, Penfield stimulated the temporal lobe of the brain and the patient reported a re-created memory of a childhood experience.

Penfield found that stimulating various areas of the cortex produces a range of responses, but that only stimulation of the temporal lobes leads to reports of meaningful and integrated experiences. These experiences are often *complete* in that when re-created they include the colour, sound, movement, and emotional content of the original experiences.

Of particular interest in these studies is the fact that some of the memories stimulated electrically by Penfield had been unavailable in normal recall. In addition to this, the stimulated experiences seemed to be far more specific and accurate than normal conscious recall which tends to be a generalization. It is Penfield's belief that the brain records *every* item to which it pays conscious attention, and that this record is basically permanent although it may be "forgotten" in day-to-day living.

That brings us roughly up to date. Looking back over history, we see that real thinking in this area has been going on for only a little over 2,500 years, and that for as many as 2,000 of those years virtually no advances were made. In fact, only a few hundred years of progressive thought have passed, and during those years man has progressed from thinking of memory in terms of spirits and vague concepts to tracking it down to a fairly small area of the body.

But even now, he is still only at the beginning of his search. Every month more than 80 new articles are published from the major research centres in the world. It may not be long before the next major advance is made.

PERSONAL NOTES

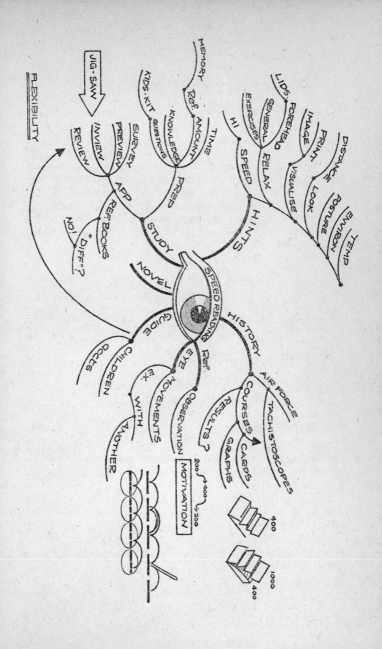

6. Note-Making and Fast Writing

Concise and efficient note-making has been a problem for everyone who has gone through the normal school system. This chapter outlines traditional note-making methods and presents the latest evidence for the effectiveness of new key word note-making techniques. In addition to this, advice is given on more creative and flowing note-making, as well as on abbreviation techniques and the solution of physical problems in fast writing.

KEY WORD SUMMARY

Traditional methods

Speed

Key words

Creative note-making

Abbreviation

The physical process

Traditional Methods

Stenography, a term which used to cover only shorthand techniques, now covers a wide range of techniques devoted to getting essential information down in the most efficient way possible.

The most popular method to date has indeed been the shorthand system, which by abbreviating the symbols for letters and words, enabled people to write as fast as they could speak. A number of people still learn shorthand for school, college and university to ensure they miss none of the lecturer's words of wisdom.

Studies on Key Words

Recently, this approach has been strongly questioned, where the purpose of taking notes is learning and recall.

Dr Gordon Howe at Exeter University and others have done repeated studies on different kinds of note-making, and have noticed an interesting trend which can be summarized in the rather paradoxical statement: notes yes, but the fewer the better. The different note-making techniques were, in reverse order of merit, ranked as follows:

1. No notes at all (the worst technique).

2. Complete transcript notes given by the lecturer or teacher, etc.

3. Complete transcript notes made by the person learning.

4. Summary sentence notes given by the lecturer or teacher.

5. Summary sentence notes made by the learner.

6. Key word notes given by the lecturer or teacher.

7. Key word notes made by the learner.

In this last category it was also found that, within reason, the fewer key words, the better. Key words were defined as those which incorporated the most relevant sense in the shortest way possible, and which also were those words which gave the most immediate recall when the notemaker was tested. They were figuratively described by one student as being like the stepping stones one needs for a path over a swamp, the swamp being the mass of grammar-words which contain the key words, but which are themselves not essential for recall.

This finding was initially surprising, but after investigation the reason became clear. Our minds, despite what we have previously thought, do not basically recall in sentences, but recall in key words and images. Of the words we hear, speak and see, only 1-10% are these essential key words.

To prove to yourself that your mind does not work basically with sentences, jot down on a spare piece of paper all the sentences of 10 words or more that you can recall having spoken, read, or heard *during your entire lifetime*. (These should be general sentences, and not ones that you have purposely learned by repetition, such as songs and poetry.) Try this exercise before reading on.

You will probably find that you are able to get only a very few. Does it surprise you to learn, however, that the range of sentences you have encountered is numbered in the tens of millions?

Another exercise for checking on the way in which your brain works is to think about how, inside your head, your thoughts are organized when you are telling someone about a special event or circumstance. Do the sentences line up in long queues waiting to get out? No, you have in your mind pictures of the important objects, and key words, and around these you construct whatever sentences you need to express your thoughts.

Again, before reading on, go back to the previous chapter, and check over your best recall notes. If you are like 90% of the population, you will probably have written these out neatly and in sentences. Knowing now that best recall notes are ideally in key words, take a coloured pen or pencil and circle only those words which you now recognize as keys to your recall. When you have circled the key words, count the total number of words you wrote down, then add up the total number of key words you have finally selected. Work out the percentage by dividing the small number by the large number and multiplying by 100.

Creative Note-Making

Making key word notes eliminates 90% of the unnecessary note-making, and thus improves your effective writing/note-making speed by as much as 10 times. In addition to this advantage, your recall will also be greatly improved, because it will not have to waste time sifting through all the unnecessary words.

More advanced techniques can help you to recall even better. Referring back to the information we discovered about our memory, we can use the fact that we recall things which are linked and things which are outstanding, to make notes which are many times more effective than even the best standard key word notes.

Using arrows, colours, and special codes, you can make connections between your key words which immediately show you where the relationships lie. This is far superior to lines or lists of key words, which give you the essence but do not show you the relationship between the ideas.

To make these newly-linked key words and images even easier to recall, you can make them outstanding.

This can be done in various ways, including:

> colour
>
> three-dimensionalizing
>
> size variation
>
> outlining
>
> underlining

Making notes in this way will enable you to speed up even more, for you will not need as much repetition as even the best key word note-maker sometimes finds necessary. These new notes will develop in front of you a mental map of information, improving all aspects of your mental performance.

By referring to the "brain patterns" at the end of each chapter, you will find examples of all the above techniques, and will see how effective they are for assisting your recall.

Having reached a stage where your note-making gives the essence, and does not concern itself with unnecessary and irrelevant words, you will already be a far "speedier" note-maker than the average. You can increase this ability even more by using some of the techniques that originally inspired formal shorthand writing.

Abbreviations

Knowing that the words you have are essential, you can begin
to abbreviate even these. One of the most effective methods is
to write the word without vowels, and using only the
consonants. It is surprising how readily your eye will recognize
the outline. Fr xmpl I m sr y wll hv no dffclty rdng ths bbrvtn.

Physically Speeding Up

You can speed up your writing by giving yourself practice
sessions at writing faster. The average writer can record
somewhere between 25 and 35 five-letter words per minute.
By giving yourself one minute practice "speed sessions" you
will find that you can considerably improve on this.

To achieve increased speed and maintain it over long
periods of time, you must avoid the danger of writer's cramp
and muscular tension. A reasonably relaxed and upright
posture is far better than the scrunched-up hunch-shouldered
collapse that many of us get ourselves into. In addition, as with
other areas mentioned in this book, it is far better to have a
smooth regular flow of activity than to have an occasional
muscularly tense and more rigid spurt.

Extending Your Note-Making

One exciting aspect of this new form of patterning notes is that
it allows you to develop other mental areas in addition to
recall. This applies particularly to developing your creative,
organizational and presentation abilities. It is on these areas
that the next chapter concentrates.

PERSONAL NOTES

7. Creativity

Most people possess a much greater creative ability than they have ever thought possible. This chapter, referring back to the chapters on the brain and on memory, indicates that traditional methods of testing creativity are inadequate. New explanations for creative thinking are given, and an original approach to creative thinking is touched on in the brain pattern section.

KEY WORD SUMMARY

> Self estimates
>
> A creativity test
>
> Standard interpretations
>
> Brain structure
>
> Memory
>
> Standard testing
>
> Two aspects
>
> Exercise
>
> Brain patterns

A CREATIVITY TEST

On a separate piece of paper, give yourself *exactly two minutes* to write down, as fast as you can, all the different uses you can think of for an ordinary paperclip. When you have finished the exercise, and *only* when you have finished, turn the page.

Score this test by adding up the total number of uses
thought of, and dividing by 2 to give you an average number
of uses thought of per minute. (The average score ranges
between 2 and 8.) It is a standard test given in schools,
universities and large business organizations to determine
"inherent creative capacity". After reading the following
information about creativity you will realize that your
inherent creative capacity is far greater than this simple test
could possibly measure, and that there are easy and relaxing
ways of releasing the potential you have.

Creativity and Your Brain's Structure

Creativity, of all the mental areas, is that one in which most
people rank themselves especially low. This is not surprising,
because as you have realized from the chapter on the use of the
brain, the "creative brain", for want of a better expression, is
generally left out of education. Any activity which involves
imagination, colour, rhythm, or form has been traditionally
frowned upon as "less intelligent". Fortunately we now have
more information to work with, and creativity can be seen as a
necessary part of a well-balanced education and personality.

The Fallacy of Standard Testing

The test in which you were asked to think of as many uses as
you could for a paperclip is one of the traditional tests given to
measure this aspect of our intellect. The faults of this test were
of two main kinds. First, it assumed creative ability to be
simply quantitative — i.e. dependent on the *number* of uses a
person could think of; and secondly, even in the quantitative
area it was weak. It did not actually measure the "basic or
innate" capacities that it purported to measure — that is,
creativity. Instead it measured how inadequately the brain
had been taught to combine language and imagination.

The irrelevance of this test can be seen by picturing an
imaginary Brain Salesman who is trying to convince an
audience that they must "buy brains". He tells them he has the
most amazing product ever and he has three pieces of
information, all academically valid, that will convince them
they must buy.

First he explains the physiology of the brain in detail, closing on the emphatic point that the number of patterns that can be formed in any single brain is 1 followed by 10 million kilometres of noughts.

Secondly, he points out that the simple mnemonic memory techniques show that the human brain can link any object with any other object; for if it could not, these systems, which worked for centuries, would immediately fail.

And, thirdly, he states that his fantastic product can, when put under pressure, think of as many as six uses for a paperclip in a minute!

When these three facts are placed next to each other, it becomes obvious that *something* must be seriously wrong with our standard creativity test, and this indeed turns out to be the case.

The Quantitative Aspect of Creativity

All that the test measures is the rigidity with which the person being tested has been taught to use language, especially words like "uses". The more rigidly taught mind will assume that "uses" refers to ordinary, sensible applications of a paperclip. The less rigidly taught mind, and the one which consequently will be regarded as more creative, will find more expansive interpretations of the word "uses", and consequently will come up with many more applications for the paperclip. The creative genius will break all the ordinary boundaries, and will include in his list many "far out" applications such as melting a few billion of them down to form the shell of a space-ship.

The creative mind is expanding his connections for the word "uses" to include the phrase "connections with".

Realizing that this is the proper method of performing in a creativity test, and checking back to confirm that the mind can make a virtually limitless series of connections, linking any one thing to anything else, we realize that our score on the creativity test can immediately go off the top of the chart.

So that you can prove this for yourself, 40 items have been listed on page 114, for you to associate with the concept "paperclip". When you, or you and your friends, have completed this series of associations, see if there is anything in the universe you can think of which you or a friend cannot in some way or other connect with the idea of a paperclip. It will be a life-long task.

orange	pigeon	water
watch	bottle	holiday
window	shoe	dinner
leaf	book	garage
table	cup	tea
radio	cloud	tree
lightbulb	pepper	house
handbag	glass	wine
pen	chair	maid
tyre	garden	newspaper
ear	Germany	pub
potato	wood	banana
kitchen	rain	mirror

For some of these you will be able to find connections immediately, others may at first seem obscure and impossible. In the end you will find they can all be connected to "paper-clip" in some way, as did the person who connected them all except "pigeon". This he was convinced had no connection, until a friend suggested using a paperclip to fix an important message on to the pigeon's leg.

Once you realize this almost limitless quantitative creative ability, you will be able to write as many uses for a paperclip as your hand can physically write in a minute. This will mean that the test is measuring not your creative ability, but your writing speed.

If you are allowed to speak your answers, you can generate between 150 and 200 in a minute, and once again the test would not be measuring your creative power, simply your ability to speak at speed.

At this stage, when you are producing 200 or more uses per minute, in comparison to the average of between 2 and 8, it becomes obvious that far more information about the complex operations of our brains will be needed before we can assume that we know enough to measure even *one* aspect of its extraordinary capacities.

The Qualitative Aspect of Creativity

Apart from the quantitative side of creativity, there is another side generally omitted from tests like the one discussed. The second area of creativity is the qualitative. This includes such things as order, relevance, simple connectivity, complex connectivity, and an overall sense of completeness and harmony.

The qualitative aspect of creativity can be very well expressed in the brain pattern form introduced in the previous chapter. If you wish to generate a large number of ideas, while at the same time giving them order and form, the brain pattern allows you to do this with exceptional ease, permitting you to organize, as well as to recall completely, your own personal "brain storming" session. It can also be done in a group.

An Exercise in Creativity

In the centre of a page draw an image of the thing around which you wish to generate your creative ideas. Working with speed uppermost in your mind, branch off from the centre, connecting ideas wherever they "fit in" as fast as they come into your head.

When doing this activity, it is best to keep a single word per line, as each word has its own massive series of associations and if kept separate will tend to "spark off" more ideas and images than it will do if trapped in a phrase or sentence. Images and words on the branches near the centre are usually the primary ideas, and the less primary ideas branch out towards the boundary of your pattern. Sometimes, however, you will notice that a given idea or image pops up all over the place at the extremes, and because of this omni-presence you will realize that it is perhaps the underlying concept with which you are really concerned.

It is also important when generating these ideas to print the letters separately. This is because your eye will be able to see them far more immediately than if they are in connected handwriting. In this speedy generation of ideas the advantage of immediate and clear vision will outweigh the disadvantage of the slightly longer time taken for printing.

Brain Patterns

From this chapter you will by now realize that the way to prepare and organize your thoughts for most purposes is not in sentence or list form. The most appropriate way is to use a creative brain pattern, for not only will the ideas generated be far more numerous, they will also automatically fall into their own connected and sensible order.

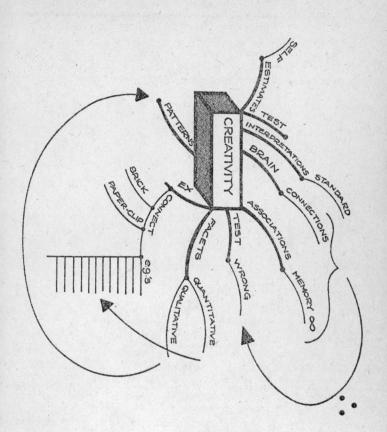

PERSONAL NOTES

8. Numeracy

Although many people have a fear of numbers, the latest information on the brain indicates that everyone has an enormous basic mathematical ability. Part of this research has shown that your brain divides work between the mathematical side and the non-mathematical side. The bulk of this chapter deals with special and easier ways of handling addition, subtraction, multiplication and division.

KEY WORD SUMMARY

> Fear
>
> Basic capacity
>
> Your brain and mathematics
>
> Addition
>
> Subtraction
>
> Multiplication
>
> Division
>
> Enjoying mathematics

Fear of Numbers

"Mathematics", "calculation", "algebra", "fractions", "long division", "subtraction", "multiplication", "addition" and many other similar words referring to the world of numbers, give little twinges of fear to more than half the people who hear them.

Why?

It is fortunately not because we have a basic inability in this area, but because we have been "trained away" from mathematics. At school, the mathematical subjects are often described as "academic", "difficult", and "only for the real brains". In the early stages many children become bored very quickly with reciting tables over and over again, and many

119

others, having failed over some of their first calculations, assume that they are "no good" at it and concentrate on other subjects.

Adding to the problems that we have with mathematics is the still widely held assumption that numbers are a particularly male preserve. In many schools, girls used to be discouraged from going on with mathematics, a decision that certainly placed them at a disadvantage and which was based on social attitudes rather than on fact:

Your Amazing Latent Mathematical Capacity

We now know that there are four main factors which determine mathematical ability, and these are based not on race or sex, but on:

1. techniques

2. practice

3. memory

4. brain's basic ability

1. TECHNIQUES. Over the years mathematicians have developed increasingly easy techniques for dealing with different forms of mathematical calculation. These are now more readily available, and those who use them are inevitably better "calculators" than those who do not. This chapter outlines, with examples, some of the more basic techniques.

2. PRACTICE. All good calculators, especially those considered "great", admitted that their skill was achieved not only by techniques but also by continual practice—none was just "able to juggle with numbers". As with other mental areas, the ability to calculate is a skill, and requires practice to enable the brain to become familiar with the various aspects of the task.

3. MEMORY. Without exception, the great calculators committed to memory many of the fundamental techniques and formulae necessary to their art. Previously, this was seen

as an insurmountable barrier by those who thought that the
memory had a limited capacity. As you will now have learnt
from the chapter on memory, each one of us has an almost
limitless memory, and if your memory is used properly it will
find all memory tasks relatively easier, including mathematics.

4. THE BRAIN'S BASIC ABILITY. In the same way as we in
the past underestimated the capacity of memory, so we
underestimated the general ability of the brain. It was
assumed that some people were basically capable in
mathematics, and that others were not, no matter how much
assistance they were given. What we now know, of course, is
that the brain has an almost limitless capacity, and that this
ranges over all the subjects, including the "sciences" and
"arts". Professor Ornstein's research on the left and right
halves of the brain has also shown that each of us has a
"mathematical" brain and an "imaginative" brain, and that
our potential in each is basically equal. Any "disability" that
we may have is probably due to our leaving that area
untended, rather than to any basic fault in the working of the
brain.

Weakness in mathematics may also stem from early ability
being dampened. One six-year-old boy, for example, was
always able in his mathematics class to give the teacher
answers to maths questions the minute the teacher had
finished asking. The boy never wrote anything down, and as a
consequence was told that what he was doing was "wrong". He
thought about this for a few days, and came into the class
saying that he used "moon numbers" to do the calculations in
his head. Moon numbers, it turned out, was his name for
special numbers that he used to reduce other large numbers to
more simple units. He would then juggle with the simple units,
converting the final unit to a large number which gave him the
correct answer. He called them "moon numbers" because
someone had told him about the solar system and the stars,
and he thought that if the numbers were "wrong" they must
have come from outside the earth. He was eventually
pressured to stop using them, as parents complained that the
entire class was being dragged along too fast and the other
children were unable to keep up.

These four "qualifications" for becoming a good calculator indicate that virtually everyone can do it. If anyone is still in doubt, and insists that "I know that I would never be able to do calculation and mathematics," it should be pointed out that if they could not do mathematics they would not be alive. For our brains are doing the most incredible series of mathematical calculations and computations during nearly every second of the day.

During every waking moment your eyes are "calculating" with millions of tiny bits of light-information. These bits of information continually add, subtract, blend, and multiply, depending on your attention, motivation and state of general awareness.

Simultaneously, that part of the brain which handles your hearing is mathematically discriminating between the millions of different nuances in sound, while also working on a complicated formula that adds and multiplies the intensity of the soundwaves in order to give you an idea of loudness.

While all of this is going on, your brain is making sure that the number of electro-chemical reactions in your brain every moment (a number between 100,000 and 1 million) is perfectly balanced, while also calculating that the number of heartbeats and breaths per minute is exactly right for the body's fuel and energy needs.

And finally, while all of *that* is going on, you may be choosing for yourself the largest portion of pie (an instantaneous geometrical calculation of a three-dimensional object's size and volume in space) and eating it (an activity which requires your brain to calculate the weight, volume, velocity, and direction of yet another three-dimensional object in space, making sure that it is directly on target).

When you consider all this, it becomes obvious that everyone is "good at mathematics" whether he or she likes it or not. So rather than wasting time on false premises and fears, let us get on with the job of showing your brain, which *can* do it, how to deal with some of the basic techniques for improving its mental arithmetic and its ability to add, subtract, multiply and divide.

An Example of Quick Calculation

If you wish to subtract a number from a number such as 100, 1,000, 10,000, 100,000, and 1,000,000, *do not* work from the right in the traditional manner.

Work from the *left* to the *right* subtracting each individual number from 9, and the last one from 10.

For example, if you want to subtract 76 from 100, you take 7 from 9 which is 2, and 6 from 10 which is 4, giving the correct answer: 24.

If we want to subtract 527 from 1,000, we work from the left, subracting 5 from 9 which is 4, 2 from 9 which is 7, and 7 from 10 which is 3, giving us 473.

If we wish to subtract 792 from 10,000 we subtract 0 from 9 which is 9, 7 from 9 which is 2, 9 from 9 which is 0 and 2 from 10 which is 8, giving again the correct answer: 9,208.

As you can see, you subtract the lower number only from the noughts, and not from the one. If your lower number is much smaller than the large number, then you add noughts to the lower number until it reaches the farthest left nought of the high number, as we did in the last calculation which was taking 0792 from 10,000.

Another way of looking at this method is to say that when subtracting from, say, 1,000 we change that number to 999 for the moment, then finally add 1 to compensate.

9	9	9	9
-0	-7	-9	-2
9	2	0	7
			+1
9	**2**	**0**	**8**

With only a minimum amount of practice you can develop this mental arithmetic into an almost instant answer, and can often, if challenged by others, get to the stage of giving them the answer almost as they give you the question.

Try this technique both by writing your numbers and answers down, and then by doing them "in your head".

Addition

Among the many techniques for addition, there are four which make the basic process considerably easier:

    1. 10-packets

    2. complete 10s

    3. multiples

    4. splitting the numbers

10-PACKETS. Whenever adding long columns of numbers, always look for the "10-packets". For example in the following addition:

        57
        58
        33
        91
        72
        46
        19
        64

it is a waste of time to add them up by mumbling to yourself 9 plus 4 is 13, plus 6 is 19, plus 2 is 21, plus 1 is 22 and so on.

It is far easier to link the numbers that make 10, giving you a series of 10-packets.

By quickly and lightly striking through the 10-packets with a pencil, you do not lose track of the ones you have already packeted. Thus in the column we are considering, the 7 and the 3 make a 10, the 8 and the 2 make a 10, the 1 and the 9 make a 10, and the 6 and 4 make a 10, giving us an easy calculation of 40. In the next column the 5 and the 5 make a 10, the 3 and the 7 make a 10, the 9 and the 1 make a 10, and the 4 and the 6 make a 10, which when we add the 4 from the other column gives us 440.

Try it with the next addition problem:

$$93$$
$$28$$
$$32$$
$$86$$
$$61$$
$$17$$
$$44$$
$$22$$

In the units column the 3 and the 7 make a 10, the 8 and the 2 make a 10, and the 6 and the 4 make a 10, giving 3 tens with 3 left over: 33. In the next column the 9 and the 1 make a 10, the 8 and the 2 make a 10, and the 6 and the 4 make a 10 with 5 left over to which we add the 3 from the previous column, giving a total of 383.

Putting numbers in 10-packets can often double the speed of your calculations.

COMPLETE 10'S. You take the 10-packet technique one step further by combining two-digit numbers that form multiples of 10. This technique can be seen clearly from the following example:

$$34$$
$$26$$
$$97$$
$$15$$
$$13$$
$$55$$

By blending these in an easy manner, we can break this column down into: 34 and 26 make 60; 97 and 13 make 110; 15 and 55 make 70. Then 60 plus 110 plus 70 equals 240.

As with 10-packets, this technique can often reduce by one half the time you spend on a lengthy calculation

MULTIPLES. When you are faced with a long column of numbers, it is often useful to check down the entire column, seeing how many numbers there are which are repeated. Your addition problem can then be made simpler by applying the multiplication tables to what initially appeared to be a large and threatening addition problem.

For example:

```
7
8
6
1
5
7
7
9
6
5
1
5
9
9
8
7
8
```

Lightly marking off the numbers which are repeated, we find that there are three 9s, three 8s, four 7s, two 6s, three 5s and two 1s. The problem can therefore be written out in this form:

$$3 \times 9 = 27$$
$$3 \times 8 = 24$$
$$4 \times 7 = 28$$
$$2 \times 6 = 12$$
$$3 \times 5 = 15$$
$$2 \times 1 = 2$$

The addition then becomes a far simpler one, and the correct answer of 108 is more easily found.

The example given here is a fairly short addition problem, but the more numbers there are to be added, the more useful becomes the technique of multiples.

SPLITTING THE NUMBERS. Suppose you were given the following addition problems:

$$
\begin{array}{cc}
31 & 425 \\
54 & 379
\end{array}
$$

You could accomplish them by mental arithmetic if you "split the numbers". All that this implies is that you separate the numbers into two smaller parts, making a "hard" addition comparatively easy. Once you have done this the addition can be done with amazing simplicity.

In the first example we split the numbers 31 and 54:

$$
\begin{array}{cc}
3 & 1 \\
+5 & +4 \\
\hline
8 & 5
\end{array}
$$

Seen like this the answer 85 is more immediately obvious.

This splitting-the-number technique becomes even more useful with larger numbers. In the second example, again we split them into two more easily manageable numbers:

$$
\begin{array}{cc}
42 & 5 \\
+37 & +9 \\
\hline
79 & 4 \\
+1 & \\
\hline
80 &
\end{array}
$$

The first simple addition gives us 14, from which we carry the 1 to the other addition. The two additions combine to give the answer 804.

Splitting the numbers, especially when applied to more difficult additions, can improve your speed of calculation, often by as much as 5 times. This technique and the others can all be improved by special practice and in particular by enjoyable "mathematical games" which lead to ever-increasing facility and enjoyment with numbers. A few of these are outlined at the end of the chapter.

Subtraction

There are two main techniques for making subtraction easier:

1. add
2. splitting the numbers

ADD. Take an example like the following:

7596
4779
—————

Most people will go through a process something like: "9 from 6 won't go, borrow, 9 from 16 is 7, carry the 1, and so on". Rather than performing what in the end could be a fairly laborious process, it is far easier to apply addition to the subtraction problem. Before you start, "prepare" the numbers in the following way. If a number above is smaller than the number below, you automatically add 10 to it and add 1 to the lower figure in the next column to the left. The subtraction is then done by reciting the number you need to add to each lower number in order to make up the number above it.

Thus in the example given, the subtraction will be done in the following way: the 5 and the 6, being smaller than the 7 and the 9, will be made into 15 and 16:

7	15	9	16
5	7	8	9

Speaking the answer to yourself as you go, you will recite: "9 plus 7 is 16, 8 plus 1 is 9, 7 plus 8 is 15, 5 plus 2 is 7."

By using this method you will have arrived at the correct answer, 2817, in a more rapid manner than by the traditional method.

In long subtractions, you can save an enormous amount of time with this approach of preparing the number before you start to subtract and then "adding" to find the correct answer.

SPLITTING THE NUMBERS. As with addition, subtraction can also be done more easily if larger numbers are split up into smaller ones. Imagine that you are given the following subtractions:

97	154	528
-32	-42	-212

In the first example we split the numbers 97 and 32 into:

9	7
-3	-2
6	5

Seen like this the answer 65 is once again more immediately obvious.

The two more "difficult" examples can be similarly split up, and it can be seen that the answers are almost immediately available.

15	4
-4	-2
11	2

52	8
-21	-2
31	6

In subtractions where the lower number has individual numbers in it that are larger than the individual number they are being taken away from, simply make the appropriate adjustments of adding tens and giving ones to the next column when splitting the numbers. To subtract 247 from 393, prepare the numbers like this:

39	13
25	7
14	6

OTHER METHODS. In addition to adding and splitting, there are other techniques in subtraction which you may explore in specialist books written on rapid calculation. The technique for quick calculation mentioned earlier in the chapter is an example of one of these more advanced approaches.

Multiplication

In multiplication there are two especially useful techniques:

> 1. multiplying by 5
> 2. multiplying by 11

MULTIPLYING A NUMBER BY 5. To multiply a number by 5 we multiply by 10 and then divide by 2. So to multiply 5 times 84,580 we simply add a nought (which is the same as multiplying by 10) to get 845,800; then we divide by 2 to get the answer 422,900.

This method saves a lot of time and is even more useful when combined with the "group vision" technique for dividing numbers, as explained in the division section below.

MULTIPLYING A NUMBER BY 11. To multiply a two digit number by 11, add the two digits together and put their sum in the middle.

For example, if we want to multiply 72 by 11, we split the 7 and 2 and put in the middle the sum of 7 and 2: 9, giving us 792 as the answer.

If the sum of the digits comes to 10 or more, simply add 1 to the left digit: for example, if we wanted to multiply 85 by 11 we would split the 8 and the 5, add them to give 13, giving us the answer 935.

In the same way that this technique suddenly becomes easy, so there is an enormous range of quick calculation techniques for multiplying longer numbers by 11, multiplying numbers by 15, 25, 50, 75, 125, and others. And for those who are exceptionally interested, there are also techniques for the cross multiplication of large numbers.

From the simple devices so far exemplified, it should be increasingly clear that mathematical ability depends on knowing how to do it — and there *are* methods.

Division

Two easy methods immediately present themselves for:

> 1. division by 2
>
> 2. division by 5

DIVISION BY 2. To divide numbers by 2, apply "group vision". This means splitting the number into easily manageable sections, as we did with addition and subtraction. For example, to divide the number 6,728,544 by 2 we simply split it up in the following way:

6   72   8   54   4

Each of these numbers is easily divisible by 2, and running through them in order we get the answer 3, 36, 4, 27, 2: 3,364,272.

This little example indicates that anyone who wishes to become a rapid calculator must learn to scan numbers before getting involved too deeply in them. When you are dividing by 2, split up the number by means of small strokes or dashes — although as you progress you will normally find that a look will be sufficient. This group vision, while applying in particular to division by 2, is also a useful general principle in quick calculation.

DIVISION BY 5. To divide any number by 5, divide by 10 and double it.

For example, 823 divided by 5 equals 82.3 multiplied by 2, equals 164.6.

As with the other mathematical procedures, there are many different techniques for dividing. The ones shown here are simply indications of the easier path that is available.

Further Helpful Hints

As well as specific calculating techniques, there are a number of aids which will help to improve your ability with numbers:

1. READING WITH A GUIDE. If you have ever seen an expert mathematician or accountant adding columns of numbers, you will have noticed that he guides his eyes down the columns by use of either his finger or a pencil. Sophisticated calculators use the guide because it helps their eyes maintain direction and concentration, as well as helping to maintain a more effective "group vision". Whenever you are doing calculation, it is advisable to use such a guide, preferably a pencil which will enable you to make appropriate markings.

2. IMAGINE. The great calculators have emphasized that when performing their calculations they try to stop themselves from muttering, mumbling, or mentally sounding the numbers. Their technique is always to "see" the numbers and answers in their mind's inner eye. This technique takes a little time to improve, but always works. Referring to the chapter on the make-up of your brain, you will see that the calculators are using the "right side" of their brains to imagine the correct answer more clearly. Practising in this way, therefore, has the advantage of enabling you to calculate very quickly and at the same time is a useful exercise for developing the mental abilities of your right brain.

3. PLAYING MATHEMATICAL GAMES. Three useful games for sharpening up your mental calculating ability are the "Hundred Complement" and the "Double" and the "Half" games.

You say "Hundred Complement" to your partner and throw him 68; he then has to throw back 32. Then he throws a number under 100 to you—for example 26—and you have to throw back 74. There are all kinds of ways of scoring such a game, although it can be better not to score at all but simply to enjoy the back and forth excitement of increasing speed.

The "Double" and "Half" games are similar. You throw the number 33, and your opponent has to throw back 66. He throws 95, and you have to throw back 190. Or you throw 96 and he has to throw back 48.

Throughout your entire re-education in numbers, it is important to remember that you *do* have the ability, and that the whole process can be *enjoyable* and rewarding.

PERSONAL NOTES

9. Logic and Analysis

In a world where communication is becoming increasingly important, and where day after day we are required to "get behind the words" to the truth of the statements from our political leaders, our television and radio, our newspapers and magazines, and our business and scientific advisers, it is essential for all of us to develop our capacity for logical analysis. As propaganda and persuasion techniques have become more sophisticated, so has the mental equipment needed for sorting out the wheat from the chaff. The remainder of this chapter is devoted to ten main areas in which communication can go astray, with examples, explanations of why the communication is not "true", and sections on "how to deal with it".

KEY WORD SUMMARY

> Fallacies
>
> Emotional language
>
> Appeal to authority
>
> Undefined source
>
> Changes in definition
>
> Greater good or evil
>
> No decision — no action
>
> Angering the opponent
>
> Yes, but
>
> Biased statistics
>
> Exercises and games

A logical argument is one in which, if the basic facts or premises are true, the conclusions that follow must be true.

It is usually easy enough to check the facts of any argument by referring to the source, and by asking appropriate questions about the way the facts were established. But do the arguments based on those facts lead to a logical conclusion? This is not so easy to check as it might seem, and many people have been led up the garden path by arguments that appear to be logical but are not.

There are two major forms of logical presentation and misrepresentation, and they can be stated as follows:

1. All As are B

   All Bs are C

   Therefore all As are C

2. All Bs are C

   A is a C

   Therefore A is a B

One of these is correct: the other is not.

A simple diagram of the first example will help us see that if the premise or initial statement is correct, then the final statement will also be correct. If we take the group B, and make it a circle, then the group of As will be a smaller circle within the group of B, because *all* As are B. If all Bs are C, then C will be an even larger circle than B, and as can be seen *all* As will therefore be C.

The soundness of this reasoning can be illustrated by a simple example:

1.   All ants (A) are insects (B)

       All insects (B) are six-legged (C)

       Therefore all ants (A) are six-legged (C)

Thus this form of argument is correct, *if* the premise is true. If the premise is *un*true this form of argument not only collapses, but often becomes ridiculous, as can be seen from the following example:

This diagram shows how the first logical
presentation is correct.

---

2. All berries are good to eat

The deadly nightshade is a berry

Therefore the deadly nightshade is good to eat

Although this argument is in correct logical form, it is untrue
because its first premise is false. So when listening to, or
reading, arguments, it is necessary to check that the premises
are accurate.

The next thing to check is that the logical form is correct. The second logical form mentioned on page 135 is an example of an incorrect structure. In the diagram, C once again represents the large group, and because all Bs are C, B can be shown by a smaller circle inside. A is also a C, but A could be either inside the B circle or, significantly, outside it. To reach the final stage of the argument by saying "Therefore A is a B" is to state something that *may* be true, but is not necessarily true. It is therefore a false argument.

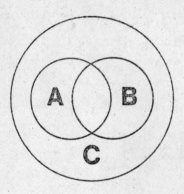

The incorrectness of this form can be seen by an example:

> All mice are four-legged animals
>
> All elephants are four-legged animals
>
> Therefore all mice are elephants

This type of argument is quite common in discussions of politics, race and religion. Forearmed with knowledge of logical structure we can help prevent such discussions from becoming unnecessarily argumentative and unproductive.

The Use of Emotional Language

Emotion in language can be used to the reader's disadvantage or advantage.

It is used to disadvantage when the speaker or writer attempts to colour the interpretation of basic facts with his own bias. For example, reporters of political events will often refer to leading politicians in terms which persuade the hearer to one view or another, but which are founded only on personal bias. If the politician is favoured, his familiar first name will be used, and the words associated with him will be "positive". The reverse will be done for the politician who is out of favour. For example, "Jim suggests . . ." is far more likely to make us feel pleasantly towards the man than "The Prime Minister demands . . ."

This persuasive use of emotional language can occur even in scientific journals. Experiments that support the work of the writer of an article will be referred to as "elegant", "sophisticated", and "excellent", whereas experiments which are in opposition to the writer's work will be labelled with such emotionally derogative terms as "sloppy", "haphazard", and "ill-conceived".

In any instance where emotional language is used, it is best to listen to the entire message, and then to separate the emotion from the fact.

Emotional language can also be used advantageously, especially in areas such as good prose writing or poetry. In these situations it is the emotion of the language that produces in the reader's mind those images which the writer especially intended to convey to him. To convert such works into pure facts would totally defeat their purpose, as was humorously pointed out by Robert Thouless in his book *Straight and Crooked Thinking*. He used for his example a couplet from the "Eve of St. Agnes", a poem by the English poet John Keats:

For on this casement shone the wintry moon,
And threw warm gules on Madeline's fair breast.

Taking the emotion and poetry from these lines, Thouless ended up with the fairly bare and singularly unpoetic lines:

For on this window shone the wintry moon
Making red marks on Jane's uncoloured chest.

In summary, emotional language can be used both to the
reader's advantage and disadvantage, and it is best for him to
know *how* the emotion is being used and, just as importantly,
why.

Arguments which Appeal to Authority

Arguments of this sort use the established reputation of a man,
a group of men, an organization, or some aspect of the media,
as "proof" that some thing or some idea must necessarily be
true. While such authority is always a useful reference, it can
be used only as a *probability* and never, in isolation, as a
proof.

Statements such as "Well, I read it in the newspaper, so it
must be true", or "Well, Professor X, Professor P, Professor Y,
and Professor Z all say the same thing as I am saying, therefore
I *must* be right", are all too commonly used in both personal
and public discussion and debate. The trouble is that even
experts and authorities are often at fault.

History has shown that in retrospect virtually every expert
has been superseded by someone who had an even wider
vision. This itself is enough to warn us of arguments which
appeal to authority, as are the frequent instances where two
experts on the same subject find themselves in total
disagreement.

When faced with such arguments, it is always important to
note the authorities being quoted, and then to check *what was
said*.

Arguments from an Undefined Source

Arguments of this sort usually assume a solid foundation, but
when the argument is looked at more closely, it can be found
that there is none.

The source may be *apparently* specific: "experts agree",
"reliable sources inform", "someone in a position of
authority". Or it may be more general: "everybody knows",
"the people of Ireland feel", "it is a commonly accepted fact
that . . . ".

Each of these arguments is making assertions on bases that are at most weak and may be completely unfounded.

Whenever confronted with such arguments, it is best to pause and ask "*What* experts?" "*Which* reliable sources?" "*Does* everybody know?" and "*Who* says that *all* the people feel?".

A humorous example showing that even the most reliable sources are sometimes at error concerns an Irish Finance Minister, whose health gave concern to three major European newspapers.

The first reported:

> The budget was delivered by Mr. Lynch, deputizing for Mr. Haughey, in hospital with concussion after hitting his head on a beam earlier yesterday.

The second newspaper was also concerned, and reported:

> Mr. Charles Haughey was knocked unconscious by a piece of gutter which fell from the roof of his house shortly before he was due to make his budget speech today.

A third newspaper completed Mr. Haughey's most unfortunate day:

> Mr. Charles Haughey was taken to hospital after being thrown from a horse only hours before he was due to make his budget speech.

Changes in the Definition of Words

Many communications and discussions become bogged down because subtly and almost imperceptibly the meanings of the key words in the argument change as the argument progresses. This is especially true of discussions revolving around concepts such as "peace" and "good and evil", as well as in discussions about religion, politics and philosophy.

In such discussions one should of course attempt to define the words. At the same time we have to realize something about the basic nature of words: that rather than having absolute definitions, each word can have hooked on to it a great variety of meanings. Each person will have different associations for each word, and it is therefore important in discussion to find out exactly what meanings the other people in the discussion have hooked on to their key words. People are often surprised to find that in a group it is they and they alone who have given a word certain connections which they had previously assumed to be common.

To bring this point home, it is useful to ask a friend to think of the first six words that in his or her mind connect with words like "run", "God", "happy" and "love", and then compare them with your own first six. The disparity will be both surprising and illuminating. So far in the author's experience no two people have been found who had identical associations for *any* given word!

If this point is allowed for in discussion, far more understanding will develop. The gradual changes in the meanings of the words being used will not be taken so much as evasive or argumentative, but as a natural result of discussion, and one which can be used constructively.

Greater Good or Evil

These arguments usually take the form of "I admit that X is bad, but Y is worse, so there is no point in doing anything about X", or "I admit that X is good, but Y is better, so we may as well forget about X and concentrate on Y".

The dishonesty in these arguments is that they are based on restrictive "either—or" thinking and not on constructive "both—and" thinking. If X and Y are evil, then *both* should be dealt with. And similarly if both X and Y are good, then *both* should be encouraged.

Thus if there is a high crime rate in a city *and* housing conditions are poor, both problems can be dealt with at the same time. And if there is a need for satisfying our curiosity about space *and* a need for better medical facilities, again both can be investigated simultaneously. Even when, in those rare instances, only one course of action is possible because of

Everyone attaches different meaning-hooks to every word, as shown by these two examples from different people of associations for the word "run".

pressure of time, the "both — and" argument still applies. In these instances the most important area is dealt with first *and* the second area is then dealt with as soon as possible.

The "both — and" argument is made even stronger when it is realized that if both activities are engaged in, they usually soon begin to supplement each other. Thus in the first example better housing would automatically begin to reduce crime; and a reduction in crime would tend to lead to a more stable family life.

The investigation of space has already given many benefits to medical science, and medicine in turn has been able to protect the lives of the astronauts.

The No Decision/No Action Argument

This form of argument arises when there are two equal choices, and where it is exceptionally hard to make a choice between the two. The result is often either inability to decide either way, or an assumption that because the decision is so hard to make there is no point in making it.

It happens surprisingly often in examinations, where many people have a little discussion with themselves over which of two questions to answer, both questions having equal marks. Some students have been known to spend the entire time allowed for the question in trying to decide which one to answer! Similarly businessmen have been known to spend hours, and *even days*, shuffling papers and trying desperately to decide where to start. Sometimes they never do.

This situation can normally be clarified by realizing that there are not two choices but three:

1. to take the first option
2. to take the second option
3. to opt out

Looked at in this light, the problem becomes clear and is solved more easily. For the situation that gave rise to the two alternatives is usually one which requires action. If this is the case it can be seen that choice number three is inadequate, and that if the other two choices are so nearly equal it does not really matter which one is chosen, *as long as it is one of them.*

Many people find that in such situations it is useful to flip a coin to decide. There have been reports that having flipped a coin which dictates one choice, they suddenly realize that that really is not the one they want and are thus able to select the other.

The no decision/no action argument is valid only when no action was really desired in the first place.

Angering the Opponent

This technique of arguing, although basically dishonest, is astonishingly successful. The "angerer" finds out things that will especially annoy his opponent, begins to emphasize them, and as a result the opponent, emotionally upset, argues badly.

The answer to this kind of illogical argumentative approach, is simply to realize that it is being used. The person who is being emotionally attacked will realize that the "angerer" himself must feel threatened or weak. It is one of the principles of combat that once the person attacked realizes that the attacker is in some way weak or afraid, the attacked person immediately becomes stronger and often assumes the "controlling" role. The same applies to intellectual argument, and it is surprising just how quickly the tables can be turned.

The attacked person can make his counter attack even stronger by realizing how ridiculous the "angerer" is in his attempts at upsetting. He can relax and smile at the irrelevant performance.

The Yes . . . But Arguments

Many people have been trained to disguise a basically destructive attitude under the initially affirmative "Yes" followed by the concealed, contradictory "But". No matter what is answered to the last "but", this person will agree "yes" and then add another "but", and so on. Such arguers are not trying to find the truth of a statement, nor are they trying to extend and expand an idea, but are simply trying to "bring it down".

The way to handle such situations is simply to ask them why they are continually trying to "dampen" the conversation, or ask them, before they can come in with their next "yes . . . but", to add to and expand the concepts being discussed.

As a general principle it is normally best in conversations to add and expand until a general structure has been built and then to go through with a more analytical eye looking for any possible dangers and faults in the construction.

Arguments using Biased Statistics

Two newspapers — one favourable to the government in office, the other unfavourable — reported on unemployment.

The first, in a major headline, stated: "Unemployment Total Stays Steady". The first paragraph of the story read as follows:

> "Unemployment remained practically static during the past month when the total number of unemployed rose by 3,972 to 601,874 on November 9th, representing an unchanged percentage of 2.6."

The other paper used the banner headline: "Unemployed may reach 700,000". Underneath this heading was the lead paragraph:

> "Little by little the unemployment figures are creeping up again. This month they have once more topped 600,000, which means they are the worst November total for 30 years."

Apart from a large number of other logical dishonesties (can you spot them all?) these examples illustrate the selective use of statistics in order to bias the reader toward a certain viewpoint.

In the first article, the newspaper wished to give the impression of stability. All the possible figures were probably analysed until one was found that showed no change: the percentage.

The newspaper unfavourable to the government likewise found one specific statistic that made the issue look particularly serious.

This example helps to illustrate something more about statistics than the oft-quoted statement that "numbers always lie". It shows that if the reader knows the *ingredients* that go into the statistics presented, he will have a fairly accurate awareness of the situation and will *also* know what bias the presenter of the statistics has.

This approach to statistics makes them far more interesting, for not only do they present numerical information but they also add to the reader's knowledge of the motives behind the presentation of the material.

There are many ways in which figures can be purposely selected and biased, ranging from simple and false assumptions about averages, to the more sophisticated manipulation of graphs to make good situations look bad and bad situations look better than they really are. It is advisable for the reader who wants to get to the "truth behind the numbers" either to take a basic course in statistics, or to read some of the more elementary paperbacks on how to interpret the figures that are presented to him. Once the initial fear of statistics and numbers has been overcome, hunting down logical fallacies can be an enjoyable and rewarding pastime.

Exercises and Games

In order to keep your mind analytically "in trim", adopt one or more of the following activities:

1. Collect in a scrapbook particularly amusing or outstanding examples from newspapers and magazines, illustrating the various forms of logical fallacy.

2. In personal and group conversation "set" yourself to remain continually on the lookout for flaws in argument. This does not necessarily mean stopping somebody at the end of every sentence to point out his errors, but means keeping a more watchful eye on the trends that conversations take.

3. Occasionally, or continually, examine your own methods of presentation and communication. You will often find the most useful information about your own logical weaknesses during times of extreme anger.

4. If you have a friend or acquaintance who is particularly interested in improving logical and analytical abilities, make a pact to check each other whenever errors occur. This will keep you alert both as presenter of information and as analyst of any information being presented to you.

5. Young children, once they are shown logical fallacies, are often extremely quick to pick them out. Delightful games can be played, scoring if desired, with television and radio newscasts, and with newspapers. Members of the family score points for being the first to recognize logical fallacies in the information they are all absorbing.

6. Buy newspapers and magazines that completely contradict your own viewpoints and compare them with the newspapers and magazines you normally buy.

If these exercises and games are practised, you will become more confident, relaxed and communicative with words, and will be more able to deal with the constant barrage of slightly "crooked" thinking with which we are bombarded.

PERSONAL NOTES

Advice for the Future

You have now completed your first reading of the book, and are ready to plan your continuing mental development for the future. The following are a few items of advice that you may find helpful:

1. Leave *Make the Most of Your Mind* alone for a few days and then return to it, gently browsing through sections you have read. You have given your mind a few days' rest, which allows it to "digest" the material it has taken in. And you are re-reading earlier sections with more complete knowledge than you had when you first read them. So your understanding, comprehension, and appreciation of those sections will be considerably greater than it was the first time, and the number of ideas you will generate for your own personal progress will be that much greater. For example, on reading the section on the right and left sides of the brain a second time through, you will find that all the "hooks" concerning brain patterns, creative thinking, special memory techniques, note-making, and mathematical ability will "latch on" to the information about the brain, making it far more interesting and relevant than before.

Another thing you might do while browsing through the book is mark off all those sections which give specific advice for exercising and developing your various abilities. This will enable you to refer to the book at any time, immediately selecting those areas in which you wish to give yourself extra practice and strength.

2. Make sure that you start, immediately if possible, to practise developing the fine tuning of your senses. Practise the exercises recommended in the book and make up your own exercises to develop the natural abilities you possess, not only in seeing and hearing but also in tasting, touching and feeling.

3. Hold constantly in your mind the knowledge that the

development of your mental abilities gets easier the more you attempt it and that after the initial hurdle has been conquered the path is always open to a continuing improvement. No matter where you rate yourself at the moment, if you start even the simplest programme of self-improvement, your rewards will be guaranteed.

4. As emphasized in the chapter on Memory, review is an essential part of the learning process. Decide which areas you wish to emphasize, and make sure that you have a reasonable programme of review, the more automatic the better. The advantage of reviewing, which can't be over-emphasized, is that it not only maintains your store of knowledge but also reveals interesting connections, not previously realized, between the various bits of information that you already have in your brain.

5. If possible, organize for yourself a continuing learning plan. This can mean simply going down to the local bookshop or library and obtaining five basic introductory books on a subject that has always interested you and which you have never really given yourself the time to study. It could also mean making the decision to enrol at a further education or Open University type of course, in order to give yourself a formal structure in which to learn, as well as a specific goal.

In any such learning plan, make sure that you bring all your mental abilities to bear, motivating yourself throughout to improve not only in the knowledge that you acquire, but also in your abilities to absorb, retain and use that knowledge.

It is useful, in embarking on such a plan, to organize regular learning periods for yourself. It is also essential to "over-view" the subject you will be studying, before you go into greater depth. Rather than simply plunging in and hoping for the best, check on all available sources before starting.

These sources include the specialist magazines and journals that devote themselves to the topic of your particular interest; encyclopaedias and reference books, which give excellent overview, and often very useful in-depth treatment; associations and groups brought together because of their interest in the subject which is interesting you; and public information and clipping services, who are usually more than willing to help anyone starting a new area of study.

6. Remember also that your brain is more remarkable than had ever been thought and is very probably more remarkable than we think even now. The amazing facts about the number of interconnections, the extraordinary retention capacity, and the equal balance of academic and artistic activities have come to light only in recent years.

7. And finally remember that the brain *does* improve with age if it is fed and nurtured properly. No matter what state yours may be in at the moment, the prospect for its future is bright, as long as you decide to make it so.

The best time to make that decision is now.

PERSONAL NOTES

Further Reading

General Reading:

D. Bergamini "Universe" Time Life Series (1974)

> A beautifully illustrated book, useful for making comparisons with the mind.

L. Watson "Supernature" Hodder (1974)

> A book which extends the boundaries of modern science, with especially interesting sections on consciousness and the brain.

M. J. Moroney "Facts from Figures" Penguin (1951)

> An excellent introduction to the use of statistics with numerous examples on how statistics can be used for manipulation.

Novels:

F. Herbert "Dune" New English Library (1975)

> A futuristic novel exploring, realistically, the possibilities of expanding man's mental and physical potentials.

H. Hesse "The Glass Bead Game" Penguin (1973)

> A complex, but intriguing novel—long discussion of different approaches toward the refinement of mentality.

A. Van Vogt "World of Null-A" Sphere (1975)

A. Van Vogt "Pawns of Null-A" Sphere (1975)

> Thoughtful science fiction exploring the development of the power of the brain, as well as the relationship of consciousness to language.

Psychology/Practical:

T. Buzan "Speed Memory" David & Charles (1976)

> Dictionary of advanced memory techniques.

T. Buzan "Use Your Head" BBC Publications (1975)

> A companion volume to "Make the Most of Your Mind".

A. Luria "Mind of a Mnemonist" Cape (1969)

> A true story, by the psychologist who studied "S", the man with a perfect memory, for 15 years.

A. Huxley "The Art of Seeing" Prentice Hall (1975)

> An intelligent introduction to the ideas expounded by W. H. Bates in his work on good sight without glasses.

R. Ornstein "Psychology of Consciousness" Freeman (1972)

> A clearly written introductory text by the man who initiated the investigation of the right and left brain.

Readers who complete this book and who are interested in a more complete reading list or further information can write to the author, care of the Publisher.

Index

Vernon Coleman
Stress Control £1.25

Stress is the one constant factor besieging almost every individual in
our overcrowded, pressured and city-focused world. It causes
depression and sleepless nights, family tensions, sexual difficulties,
illnesses of every kind. Vernon Coleman, an experienced family doctor
and writer on many medical topics, explains how controlling stress can
be the way to a happier and healthier life.

medical editor-in-chief Dr Eric J. Trimmer
The Visual Dictionary of Sex £5.95

With more than 400 illustrations, many in full colour, *The Visual
Dictionary of Sex* is an authoritative, frank and practical guide to every
aspect of human sexual life. In one book, here is everything anyone
could ever want to know about sex and sexuality.

edited by Sigmund Stephen Miller
Symptoms £2.50
the complete home medical encyclopedia

The new medical encyclopedia – accurate, comprehensive, easy to use –
enabling the reader to track down any symptom of ill health and
identify, quickly and accurately, the causal disorder. *Symptoms* will
tell you exactly what is wrong, and guide you in what action to take,
whether a simple home remedy, or whether to seek advice from your
doctor.